*To Don Esteban
A few pages in to her
Best wishes
Richa[rd]*

Richard Lewis, May 2023

WRITING THE ISLE

KENT'S ISLE OF THANET
IN THE PAGES OF GREAT AUTHORS

RICHARD LEWIS

AT
Apple Town

An Apple Town Book

First published 2022
Published by Apple Town Publishing

Text Copyright © 2022 Richard Lewis

All rights reserved. No part of this book may be reproduced or utilised in any form or by any means – graphic, electronic or mechanical, including photocopying, recording, taping or information storage and retrieval systems – without prior written consent of the copyright owner. This book may not be circulated in any form of binding or cover other than that in which it is published and without a similar condition including this condition being imposed on any subsequent purchaser.

The right of Richard Lewis to be identified as the author of this work has been asserted by him in accordance with the Copyright, Designs and Patents Act 1988.

Cover by Bob Simmonds

British Library Cataloguing in Publication Data.
A catalogue record for this book is available from the British Library.

ISBN 978-0-9572204-3-0

CONTENTS

Chapter One   1
First Pages – Daniel Defoe, Jane Austen

Chapter Two   9
Margate Way – Charles Lamb

Chapter Three   17
Pages for Legends – Richard Barham

Chapter Four   33
Poetic Pages – Samuel Taylor Coleridge

Chapter Five   41
The Isle of Dickens – Charles Dickens

Chapter Six   58
Part of the Plot – Wilkie Collins

Chapter Seven   71
Sea Drama – R M Ballantyne

Chapter Eight   77
Setting for Love and Lies – Baroness Orczy

Chapter Nine   84
Cliff Steps Made Thrilling – John Buchan

Chapter Ten   102
Seaside Comedy – George and Wheedon Grossmith, Frank Richards

Chapter Eleven   112
Seen from the Air – Dennis Wheatley

Chapter Twelve   119
Bondland – Ian Fleming

Chapter Thirteen   124
This Isle, This England – John Betjeman, Paul Theroux

Afterword   133

FOREWORD

In my earlier book, *Creative Coast,* I told the story of major artists and writers who have lived on the Isle of Thanet, at least for a while. *Writing The Isle* takes a different angle. Here I examine how the Isle of Thanet has found its way into the writings of great authors over the years. The coastal towns of Margate, Broadstairs and Ramsgate, not to mention the surrounding villages, have all made appearances as the backcloth to countless episodes of a wide variety of novels, and are in evidence in a great deal of other literary works besides.

For some authors the draw to include the Isle of Thanet as a location in their writing was the creative spirit of the coast. For others it was the almost wild remoteness of the 'isle' as a world apart, a place for adventure and recklessness. For a few it was a nostalgic return to a place remembered from childhood. In some way or other, all have painted their own distinctive pictures of Thanet.

Daniel Defoe, in the 18th century, was the first literary giant to introduce the area to the reading public in any modern sense, even if not very flatteringly. But from this moment on the literary incursions to this part of the Kent coast gathered ever more momentum. In the early 19th century **Jane Austen** used Ramsgate, again perhaps slightly invidiously, as a location for episodes in *Pride and Prejudice* and *Mansfield Park.* Just a couple of decades later we see **Charles Lamb** proving to be a much more enthusiastic traveller to Thanet in his *The Old Margate Foy.* Around the same time, **The Reverend Richard Barham**, writing under the pseudonym of **Thomas Ingoldsby**, produced his famous *The Ingoldsby Legends,* which included many stories, in verse as well as prose, from places around Kent, including Margate and Minster.

Again almost contemporaneously, **Samuel Taylor Coleridge**, that great champion of Ramsgate, gives us a poetic picture of the 'aery cliffs and glittering sands' that lie between Ramsgate and Broadstairs. Progressing through the 19th century, it is impossible to miss the towering **Charles Dickens**, who early on depicted Ramsgate in *The Tuggses of Ramsgate.* Having adopted Broadstairs as his second home, he not only wrote about Broadstairs but brought the town, albeit slightly disguised, into perhaps his greatest novel, *David Copperfield.* Following on behind was that Victorian master of the suspense novel, **Wilkie Collins**, who was introduced to the Isle of Thanet by his friend, Dickens, and painted a number of local, mainly Ramsgate, scenes in his novels, including *The Law and the Lady* and *The Fallen Leaves*. The Scottish adventure story-writer **R M Ballantyne**, an exact contemporary of Collins, adopted Ramsgate in a slightly different way, fully incorporating the seascapes he encountered off the coast there into two of his popular novels, *The Lifeboat* and *The Floating Light of the Goodwin Sands.*

Next, moving into the early 20th century, we find the famous inventor of the Scarlet Pimpernel, **Baroness Orczy**, locating an entire novel, *The Nest of the Sparrowhawk,* in the area around Acol and Minster. Hard on her heels came that other consummate story-teller, **John Buchan**, who set the finale of his *The Thirty-Nine Steps*, one of the greatest spy stories of all time, in Bradgate, the fictional name he so eruditely gave to Broadstairs. We take a small step back in time now to the end of the 19th century to examine the wonderful comedy of the brothers, **George** and **Wheedon Grossmith**. Their richly funny lampooning of lower middle class pretensions in their novel *The Diary of a Nobody* memorably included the depiction of an annual holiday in Broadstairs. Back we go into the 20th century to find another nugget of comedy set in Thanet created by that phenomenally prolific boys' author, **Frank Richards.** Identifiable Thanet scenes crop up in many of his Billy Bunter stories, and in *Billy Bunter's Double* we find the famous fat owl of the Remove lounging on the beach at Pegg Bay, Richards' name for Ramsgate and in turn a clear variation on the name of the nearby bay at Pegwell.

The name on everyone's lips in the first half of the 20th century when it came to thrillers was **Dennis Wheatley**. One of his thrillers, *Contraband*, was entirely located in the Thanet that Wheatley knew so well from boyhood, with a very real local landmark becoming the headquarters of the foreign forces of evil. In the same vein, almost as a natural progression from Wheatley's stories, we now meet **Ian Fleming**, whose hero James Bond hardly needs any introduction. Fleming knew Thanet and the Kent coast well, and it is no surprise to find Thanet and Sandwich appearing as a backdrop for a key passage in *Goldfinger*, one of the many universally known Bond novels.

We go back now to find poetic nostalgia for the life that used to be. **John Betjeman,** a poet who really understood England**,** spirits us away from the Margate of 1940 to a summer's day in the town before the war, evoking with all his gentle humour a delight in the simple pleasures that make up an English seaside holiday. Finally, then, and almost harking back to the travels of Daniel Defoe, we finish with a latter-day view of Thanet by that incisive American travel writer and novelist, **Paul Theroux**. The opening pages of his funny, brilliantly observed *The Kingdom by the Sea* show us 1980s Thanet in all its quirky glory.

An **Afterword** takes us up to the present day, and indicates some major novels that have moved the Isle of Thanet on to centre stage in the 21st century. Evidence here that the lure of the 'isle' for authors is showing no sign of abating and is, if anything, growing even stronger.

Richard Lewis
Broadstairs, 2022

Acknowledgements

First and foremost I would like to express my gratitude to author and local historian Bob Simmonds for his help, suggestions and technical expertise in the preparation of this book.

The pages from *Billy Bunter's Double* by Frank Richards (Charles Hamilton) are reprinted by permission of Penny Tweedie, the author's great-niece, and I would like to thank her for her kind interest.

The extract from *Contraband* by Dennis Wheatley is reprinted by permission of Peters Fraser & Dunlop (www.petersfraserdunlop,com) on behalf of the Estate of Dennis Wheatley.

The extract from *Goldfinger* by Ian Fleming is reproduced with permission of Ian Fleming Publications Ltd, London Goldfinger © Ian Fleming Publications Ltd 1959 www.ianfleming.com

The poem *Margate 1940* from the *Collected Poems* by John Betjeman is reprinted by permission of Hodder & Stoughton.

The Kingdom by the Sea by Paul Theroux. Copyright © Paul Theroux, 1983, used by permission of The Wylie Agency (UK) Limited.

CHAPTER ONE

FIRST PAGES

DANIEL DEFOE

Our first view of Thanet is given by that man of many parts – writer, trader, traveller, political activist, spy – **Daniel Defoe** (1660 – 1731). Defoe had visited many areas of Great Britain in his capacity as a merchant or on political missions as an undercover agent for the Tory statesman Robert Harley. He is best known today for his novels *Robinson Crusoe* and *Moll Flanders* and for his *Journal of the Plague Year* (much revisited in our day thanks to the Corona virus pandemic), but as far as financial success went his description of the component parts of Great Britain in his *A Tour Thro' the Whole of Great Britain* was on a par with his hugely popular *Robinson Crusoe*.

Daniel Defoe

The pictures Defoe paints in his *Tour* are not simply a diary account of one great journey around Britain, but a series of recollections and reflections on the many forays he had made over the years to every part of the British Isles. He was to some extent inspired by an earlier book on the composition of Britain, *Britannia*, by **William Camden** (1551 – 1623). But where Thanet is concerned Camden's entry is minimal to say the least:

Now are we come to the Isle Tanet, which the river Stour, by Bede named Wantsum, severeth from the firme land by a small channell running betweene, which river made of two divers riverlets in the woodland country called the Weald, so soone as it goeth in one entire streame, visiteth Ashford and Wye, two prety Mercat towns well knowen.

In fact, Camden's *Britannia* itself derived much of its information from the poet **John Leland's** *Itinerary*, written between 1535 and 1543, and Leland's description of Thanet fills out some early detail:

Ther hath bene a xi. paroche chyrches in Thanet, of the which iii. be decayed, the residew remayne. In the isle is very litle wodde……. Margate lyith in S. John's paroche yn Thanet a v. myles upward fro Reculver, and there is a village and a peere for shyppes, but now sore decayed. Ramesgate a iiii. myles upward in Thanet, wher as is a smaul peere for shyppis. The shore of the Isle of Thenet, and also the inward partis ful of good quarres of chalke.

However, these earlier glimpses of Thanet cannot give the historical perspective and human interest commentary later offered by Defoe.

Today Defoe is often quoted with amusement and perhaps even a secret pride by the inhabitants of Broadstairs on the town's shady past, with his judgement on the local population's work ethic, or lack of it, appearing in tourist leaflets almost as a badge of historic honour:

Bradstow (note: the original name for Broadstairs) is a small fishing hamlet of some three-hundred souls, of which twenty-seven follow the occupation of fishing, the rest would seem to have no visible means of support! I am told that the area is a hot bed of smuggling. When I asked if this was so, the locals did give me the notion that if I persisted in this line of enquiry some serious injury might befall my person.

The Isle of Thanet, as it was from the Roman Period to the Middle Ages (late 15th Century) - a true island (left)

The Isle of Thanet in Defoe's time, joined to East Kent after the silting up of the separating Wantsum Channel (right)

The following is his fuller account of this far corner of Kent, published between 1724 – 27, with a final withering word on Sandwich, included here, even though just beyond the Thanet border, for the pure devilment of it:

The shore from Whitstable, and the East-Swale, affords nothing remarkable but sea-marks, and small towns on the coast, till we come to Margate and the North Foreland; the town of Margate is eminent for nothing that I know of, but for King William's frequently landing here in his returns from Holland, and for shipping a vast quantity of corn for London Market, most, if not all of it, the product of the Isle of Thanet, in which it stands.

On the north-east point of this land, is the promontory, or head-land which I have often mentioned, call'd the North Foreland; which, by a line drawn due north to the Nase in Essex, about six miles short of Harwich, makes the mouth of the river of Thames, and the Port of London. As soon as any vessels pass this Foreland from London, they are properly said to be in the open sea; if to the north, they enter the German Ocean, if to the south, the Chanel, as 'tis call'd, that is the narrow seas between England and France; and all the towns or harbours before we come this length, whether on the Kentish or Essex shoar, are call'd members of the Port of London.

From this point westward, the first town of note is Ramsgate, a small port, the inhabitants are mighty fond of having us call it Roman's-Gate; pretending that the Romans under Julius Caesar made their first attempt to land here, when he was driven back by a storm; but soon returned, and coming on shore, with a good body of troops beat back the Britains, and fortify'd his camp, just at the entrance of the creek, where the town now stands; all which may be true for ought any one knows, but is not to be prov'd, either by them or any one else; and is of so little concern to us, that it matters nothing whether here or at Deal, where others pretend it was.

It was from this town of Ramsgate, that a fellow of gigantick strength, tho' not of extraordinary stature, came abroad in the world, and was call'd the English Sampson, and who suffer'd men to fasten the strongest horse they could find to a rope, and the rope round his loins, sitting on the ground, with his feet strait out against a post, and no horse could stir him; several other proofs of an incredible strength he gave before the king, and abundance of the nobility at Kensington, which no other man could equal; but his history was very short, for in about a year he disappear'd, and we heard no more of him since.

Sandwich is the next town, lying in the bottom of a bay, at the mouth of the river Stour, an old, decay'd, poor, miserable town, of which when I have said that it is an antient town, one of the Cinque Ports, and sends two members to Parliament; I have said all that I think can be worth any bodies reading of the town of Sandwich.

Grave of Richard Joy, 'called the Kentish Sampson', at St Peters Churchyard, St Peters, Broadstairs

In Defoe's picture of Thanet we see an allusion to the fertile fields that produced plentiful corn and to the port at Margate, used for royal disembarkations and as an outlet for shipping the corn to London. Though it has always been something of a struggle to earn a living in Thanet, there was money to be made in both husbandry and fishing, not to mention smuggling, and the area wasn't the economic black spot it would become in more recent times. Further, its heyday was yet to arrive, some fifty years after Defoe's *Tour*, with the realization by genteel society that, within fairly easy reach of London by boat, there was a seaside place at safe remove from wagging tongues, which could offer relaxation, pleasure, health and a frisson of sexual excitement. Indeed, a place where the leisured classes could let their hair down, almost paving the way for those British tourists jingling holiday pay and flinging restraint to the wind on their annual week or two in faraway Spain two hundred years later.

JANE AUSTEN

Jane Austen (1775 – 1817) was well aware of the danger Thanet posed to polite society. Ramsgate and Margate were by now fashionable seaside resorts in her day, and Austen cast her all-seeing eye on Ramsgate in 1803 when she came on a visit. Her much-loved brother Francis was posted to Ramsgate to lead a company called the 'Sea Fencibles' for the Royal Navy in case of Napoleonic invasion, and had become engaged to local girl Mary Gibson. Eager to meet her future sister-in-law, Austen duly descended on Ramsgate. Later she would write a poem celebrating Francis and Mary's marriage in 1806, entitled *Post Haste from Thanet*. However, the church where they married, St Laurence-in-Thanet, Ramsgate, is not mentioned in the poem, nor is there any other reference to Thanet except in the title. Thanet merely appears as the name of the start point for the journey to their honeymoon destination, Godmersham Park, between Ashford and Canterbury, which was the residence of another of Austen's brothers, Edward.

Jane Austen

Austen's view of Ramsgate would come in her novels *Pride and Prejudice* (1813) and *Mansfield Park* (1814). She loved the sea, but implies a hazard warning in her portrayal of Ramsgate. For her narrative in *Pride and Prejudice* she must choose a town to which that fortune-hunter and seducer of innocence, George Wickham, manoeuvres Fitzwilliam Darcy's fifteen-year-old sister Georgiana for his planned elopement. Naturally enough the distant, socially dubious and morally suspect Ramsgate is for her the obvious choice.

In a letter Darcy hands to Elizabeth Bennet, the novel's protagonist with whom he falls in love, Darcy writes to explain the unfortunate event surrounding his young sister and the wastrel George Wickham, who had a grudge against him.

From *Pride and Prejudice* (1813):

I must now mention a circumstance which I would wish to forget myself, and which no obligation less than the present should induce me to unfold to any human being. Having said thus much, I feel no doubt of your secrecy. My sister, who is more than ten years my junior, was left to the guardianship of my mother's nephew, Colonel Fitzwilliam, and myself. About a year ago, she was taken from school, and an establishment formed for her in London; and last summer she went with the lady who presided over it, to Ramsgate; and thither also went Mr. Wickham, undoubtedly by design; for there proved to have been a prior acquaintance between him and Mrs. Younge, in whose character we were most unhappily deceived; and by her connivance and aid, he so far recommended himself to Georgiana, whose affectionate heart retained a strong impression of his kindness to her as a child, that she was persuaded to believe herself in love, and to consent to an elopement. She was then but fifteen, which must be her excuse; and after stating her imprudence, I am happy to add, that I owed the knowledge of it to herself. I joined them unexpectedly a day or two before the intended elopement, and then Georgiana, unable to support the idea of grieving and offending a brother whom she almost looked up to as a father, acknowledged the whole to me. You may imagine what I felt and how I acted. Regard for my sister's credit and feelings prevented any public exposure; but I wrote to Mr. Wickham, who left the place immediately, and Mrs. Younge was of course removed from her charge. Mr. Wickham's chief object was unquestionably my sister's fortune, which is thirty thousand pounds; but I cannot help supposing that the hope of revenging himself on me was a strong inducement. His revenge would have been complete indeed.

FITZWILLIAM DARCY

In *Mansfield Park* Austen once again needs a setting for the serious social gaffe committed by one of her characters, Tom Bertram, cousin to the novel's protagonist, Fanny Price, and what better place for this than Ramsgate? Tom meets the family of his friend Sneyd in Ramsgate and, while walking, makes the mistake of thinking the younger sister is 'out' (she isn't), chatting to her as he walks, thereby offending the older sister who is 'out'. The social code involved here is largely lost to us in the twenty-first century, indeed the modern reader might even be forgiven for thinking that when someone was 'out' they were openly gay! But the social code referred to was a serious matter for polite society in Austen's day. Being 'out' then referred to girls who had finished their education, reached marriageable age and been introduced to society with a view to having a marriage offer made by a suitable bachelor.

Here is the account of the social error as recounted by Tom Bertram.

From *Mansfield Park* (1814):

"Those who are showing the world what female manners *should* be," said Mr. Bertram gallantly, "are doing a great deal to set them right."

"The error is plain enough," said the less courteous Edmund; "such girls are ill brought up. They are given wrong notions from the beginning. They are always acting upon motives of vanity, and there is no more real modesty in their behaviour *before* they appear in public than afterwards."

"I do not know," replied Miss Crawford hesitatingly. "Yes, I cannot agree with you there. It is certainly the modestest part of the business. It is much worse to have girls not out give themselves the same airs and take the same liberties as if they were, which I have seen done. That is worse than anything—quite disgusting!"

"Yes, *that* is very inconvenient indeed," said Mr. Bertram. "It leads one astray; one does not know what to do. The close bonnet and demure air you describe so well (and nothing was ever juster), tell one what is expected; but I got into a dreadful scrape last year from the want of them. I went down to Ramsgate for a week with a friend last September, just after my return from the West Indies. My friend Sneyd—you have heard me speak of Sneyd, Edmund—his father, and mother, and sisters, were there, all new to me. When we reached Albion Place they were out; we went after them, and found them on the pier: Mrs. and the two Miss Sneyds, with others of their acquaintance. I made my bow in form; and as Mrs. Sneyd was surrounded by men, attached myself to one of her daughters, walked by her side all the way home, and made myself as agreeable as I could; the young lady perfectly easy in her manners, and as ready to talk as to listen. I had not a suspicion that I could be doing anything wrong. They looked just the same: both well-dressed, with veils and parasols like other girls; but I afterwards found that I had been giving all my attention to the youngest, who was not *out*, and had most excessively offended the eldest. Miss Augusta ought not to have been noticed for the next six months; and Miss Sneyd, I believe, has never forgiven me."

"That was bad indeed. Poor Miss Sneyd. Though I have no younger sister, I feel for her. To be neglected before one's time must be very vexatious; but it was entirely the mother's fault. Miss Augusta should have been with her governess. Such half-and-half doings never prosper….."

Albion Place, Ramsgate

Ramsgate Pier and Harbour, early 1800s

We have the distinct feeling here that Austen also thought the young girl's poor upbringing ('it was entirely the mother's fault'), and Tom Bertram's consequent social error, 'bad'. Perhaps we could even infer that this was brought on by their being in Ramsgate. As a confirmatory footnote, Austen wrote in a letter to her brother Charles' wife in 1813: 'Ed Hussey talks of fixing at Ramsgate – Bad Taste!'

CHAPTER TWO

MARGATE WAY

CHARLES LAMB

Charles Lamb (1775 – 1834) was an exact contemporary of Jane Austen's, but a far more enthusiastic traveller to Thanet. He is best known for his *Essays of Elia* and for the children's book *Tales from Shakespeare*, co-authored with his sister, Mary Lamb. He was clearly not a fan of seaside resorts, but had a particularly happy holiday in Margate. He made the trip to Margate on one of the old 'hoys', small, one-masted sailing ships mainly used for freight but also taking passengers. Lamb warms to this ancient form of transport and inveighs against the more modern steam ships, with their belching smoke and pollution. In his account of his journey to Margate he gives a detailed description of the crew and some of the other passengers, delighting in the far-fetched stories of one of the more notable travellers, and including the moving story of the lad going to the Sea Bathing Hospital in the hope of a cure. Lamb's picture is an endearing introduction to Margate, and captures the very essence of all travel and all holidays: meeting new people and learning about new places.

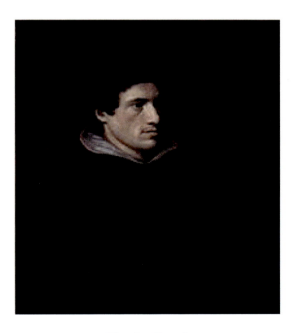

Charles Lamb

From *The Old Margate Hoy* – included in the *Last Essays of Elia* (1833):

I am fond of passing my vacations (I believe I have said so before) at one or other of the Universities. Next to these my choice would fix me at some woody spot, such as the neighbourhood of Henley affords in abundance, upon the banks of my beloved Thames. But somehow or other my cousin contrives to wheedle me once in three or four seasons to a watering place. Old attachments cling to her in spite of experience. We have been dull at Worthing one summer, duller at Brighton another, dullest at Eastbourn a third, and are at this moment doing dreary penance at–Hastings!–and all because we were happy many years ago for a brief week at–Margate. That was our first sea-side experiment, and many circumstances combined to make it the most agreeable holyday of my life. We had neither of us seen the sea, and we had never been from home so long together in company.

Can I forget thee, thou old Margate Hoy, with thy weather-beaten, sun-burnt captain, and his rough accommodations–ill exchanged for the foppery and fresh-water niceness of the modern steam-packet? To the winds and waves thou committedst thy goodly freightage, and didst ask no aid of magic fumes, and spells, and boiling cauldrons. With the gales of heaven thou wentest swimmingly; or, when it was their pleasure, stoodest still with sailor-like patience. Thy course was natural, not forced, as in a hot-bed; nor didst thou go poisoning the breath of ocean with sulphureous smoke–a great sea-chimaera, chimneying and furnacing the deep; or liker to that fire-god parching up Scamander.

Can I forget thy honest, yet slender crew, with their coy reluctant responses (yet to the suppression of anything like contempt, to the raw questions, which we of the great city would be ever and anon putting to them, as to the uses of this or that strange naval implement?) 'Specially can I forget thee, thou happy medium, thou shade of refuge between us and them, conciliating interpreter of their skill to our simplicity, comfortable ambassador between sea and land!– whose sailor-trowsers did not more convincingly assure thee to be an adopted denizen of the former, than thy white cap, and whiter apron over them, with thy neat-fingered practice in thy culinary vocation, bespoke thee to have been of inland nurture heretofore–a master cook of Eastcheap? How busily didst thou ply thy multifarious occupation, cook, mariner, attendant, chamberlain; here, there, like another Ariel, flaming at once about all parts of the deck, yet with kindlier ministrations–not to assist the tempest, but, as if touched with a kindred sense of our infirmities, to soothe the qualms which that untried motion might haply raise in our crude land-fancies. And when the o'er-washing billows drove us below deck (for it was far gone in October, and we had stiff and blowing weather) how did thy officious ministerings, still catering for our comfort, with cards, and cordials, and thy more cordial conversation, alleviate the closeness and the confinement of thy else (truth to say) not very savoury, nor very inviting, little cabin!

With these additaments to boot, we had on board a fellow-passenger, whose discourse in verity might have beguiled a longer voyage than we meditated, and have made mirth and wonder abound as far as the Azores. He was a dark, Spanish complexioned young man, remarkably handsome, with an officer-like assurance, and an insuppressible volubility of assertion. He was, in fact, the greatest liar I had met with then, or since. He was none of your hesitating, half story-tellers (a most painful description of mortals) who go on sounding your belief, and only giving you as much as they see you can swallow at a time–the nibbling pickpockets of your patience–but one who committed downright, daylight depredations upon his neighbour's faith. He did not stand shivering upon the brink, but was a hearty thoroughpaced liar, and plunged at once into the depths of your credulity. I partly believe, he made pretty sure of his company. Not many rich, not many wise, or learned, composed at that time the common stowage of a Margate packet. We were, I am afraid, a set of as unseasoned Londoners (let our enemies give it a worse name) as Aldermanbury, or Watling-street, at that time of day could have supplied. There might be an exception or two among us, but I scorn to make any invidious distinctions among such a jolly, companionable ship's company, as those were whom I sailed with. Something too must be conceded to the *Genius Loci*. Had the confident fellow told us half the legends on land, which he favoured us with on the other element, I flatter myself the good sense of most of us would have revolted. But we were in a new world, with everything unfamiliar about us, and the time and place disposed us to the reception of any prodigious marvel whatsoever. Time has obliterated from my memory much of his wild fablings; and the rest would appear but dull, as written, and to be read on shore. He had been Aid-de-camp (among other rare accidents and fortunes) to a Persian prince, and at one blow had stricken off the head of the King of Carimania on horseback. He, of course, married the Prince's daughter. I forget what unlucky turn in the politics of that court, combining with the loss of his consort, was the reason of his quitting Persia; but with the rapidity of a magician he transported himself, along with his hearers, back to England, where we still found him in the confidence of great ladies. There was some story of a Princess–Elizabeth, if I remember–having intrusted to his care an extraordinary casket of jewels, upon some extraordinary occasion–but as I am not certain of the name or circumstance at this distance of time, I must leave it to the Royal daughters of England to settle the honour among themselves in private. I cannot call to mind half his pleasant wonders; but I perfectly remember, that in the course of his travels he had seen a phoenix; and he obligingly undeceived us of the vulgar error, that there is but one of that species at a time, assuring us that they were not uncommon in some parts of Upper Egypt. Hitherto he had found the most implicit listeners. His dreaming fancies had transported us beyond the "ignorant present." But when (still hardying more and more in his triumphs over our simplicity) he went onto affirm that he had actually sailed through the legs of the Colossus at Rhodes, it really became necessary to make a stand. And here I must do justice to the good sense and intrepidity of one of our party, a youth, that had hitherto been one of his most deferential auditors, who, from his recent reading, made bold to assure the gentleman, that there must be some mistake, as "the Colossus in question had been destroyed long since;" to whose opinion, delivered with all modesty, our hero was obliging enough to concede thus much, that "the figure was indeed a little damaged." This was the only opposition he met with, and it did not at all seem to stagger him, for he proceeded with his fables, which the same youth appeared to swallow with still more complacency than ever,– confirmed, as it were, by the extreme candour of that concession. With these prodigies he wheedled us on till we came in sight of the Reculvers, which one of our own company (having been the voyage before) immediately recognising, and pointing out to us, was considered by us as no ordinary seaman.

All this time sat upon the edge of the deck quite a different character. It was a lad, apparently very poor, very infirm, and very patient. His eye was ever on the sea, with a smile: and, if he caught now and then some snatches of these wild legends, it was by accident, and they seemed not to concern him. The waves to him whispered more pleasant stories. He was as one, being with us, but not of us. He heard the bell of dinner ring without stirring; and when some of us pulled out our private stores–our cold meat and our salads–he produced none, and seemed to want none. Only a solitary biscuit he had laid in; provision for the one or two days and nights, to which these vessels then were oftentimes obliged to prolong their voyage. Upon a nearer acquaintance with him, which he seemed neither to court nor decline, we learned that he was going to Margate, with the hope of being admitted into the Infirmary there for sea-bathing. His disease was a scrofula, which appeared to have eaten all over him. He expressed great hopes of a cure; and when we asked him, whether he had any friends where he was going, he replied, "he *had* no friends."

The 'hoy' remembered in a Margate pub name

At the same time that Lamb was breezing down to Margate on the fondly remembered 'hoy', a group of writers who edited a literary magazine called *The New Monthly Magazine and Literary Journal* were printing a truly exciting picture of the ever more widely visited seaside town, one that would certainly have made Jane Austen's hair stand on end had she been alive to read it, and confirmed her worst fears about Thanet. Margate certainly sounds like a place of gay abandon in the piece. The writers on the journal were Thomas Campbell, Samuel Carter Hall, Edward Bulwer Lytton, Theodore Edward Hook, Thomas Hood and William Harrison Ainsworth. Well known and celebrated in their time and very popular, these writers seem unfamiliar to us today having sadly vanished into the margins of literary history and are no longer read – an indication indeed of how hard it is for contemporaries to predict which writers will stand the test of time. Nonetheless, their considerable merit makes them worth a quick mention here.

Thomas Campbell was a respected Scottish poet and one of the founders of University College London; Samuel Carter Hall was the Irish author of numerous books on Ireland and the Thames, also of memoirs of great people he had known; Edward Bulwer Lytton was a hugely popular and high-earning author of novels, poetry and plays – he coined a number of sayings that have entered the language, such as 'the pen is mightier than the sword'; Theodore Edward Hook was an extremely prolific author, writing a total of thirty-eight novels and even inspiring Coleridge to praise him as being "as true a genius as Dante" – praise indeed; Thomas Hood was the author of many volumes of poetry and one of the masters of memory: so many of us happily recall from school his poem 'I remember, I remember, the house where I was born'; William Harrison Ainsworth was the widely read author of a string of historical novels, often mixing fact with fiction in a way that almost prefigures the popular 'faction' of our day, with figures such as Dick Turpin, Jack Sheppard and Guy Fawkes as leading characters.

It is unclear who exactly penned this racy picture of Margate, appearing in Volume 38 of the *The New Monthly Magazine and Literary Journal* in 1833, but it certainly sells it as a fun place to visit:

...of all places of amusement in England none are like unto Margate. Here the commercial character loses its characteristics-- the trader no longer thinks of pence and shillings-- he gives himself up lavishly to the good things of life--he inquireth tenderly touching the John Dories, and, in his soul he damneth the cost. There too all are equals; the absence of the chilling sneer of the great allows the young apprentice to relax from his stiffness, and to assume the man of ton without *the dread of* being likened to the original. Sea baths in the morning prepare the appetite for shrimps and eggs; from shrimps and eggs thou passest to billiards, to pony-back, or to the reading-rooms. Then, too, to each of the baths, that, bright and newly painted, stretch seaward in a glistening row, is its own pianoforte!--some damsel gratuitously musical wakens its dulcet notes: and such pretty gay-dressed lasses escaped from Aldgate, or from the long street of Oxford, glance, giggle, laugh and coquet around, that if thou art amorous thou mayest find here the English Cadiz. Many a Jewish dark eye looks arch at thee under its flowery and feathered bonnet, for Jewesses abound at Margate. The tribes of Solomon and Levi pour forth in abundance down the sultry streets. Here, if thy name be one of gentle note, sink it, and become a Hobson or a Smith; affect no superiority; flirt and dance and laugh thy fill, and never wilt thou find thy time less heavily employed. Here what motley affluence of character, what vast miscellany of humours, greet they observing but quiet gaze! Here mayest thou find materials, ay, and adventure too, for fifty novels and five hundred plays! Whose vein shall the critics justly declare to be exhausted while Margate opens her arms to all the varieties of the most variegated classes? And beautiful is it to the philanthropist, as well as to the gallant or the observer, to behold trade thus throwing off its cares, and the reserve of the mercantile respectability blowing merrily about in the gay breezes of the pier. Some of my school-days were spent in the neighbourhood of this Omphalon Gaiæ; and well do I remember the portly president of its pleasures, that most important of all important personages--the Master of the Ceremonies! He was a character. In those good old times, ere the feudal government began to cede to the federal, Margate, Broadstairs, and Ramsgate, the triple Geryon of the coast, were united under one lordly away; now each community claimeth its own separate master of the ceremonies--the union of the three kingdoms has been repealed. Thou O Illustrious C_____! wert then supreme--defender of the faith, from the Margate assembly-room of Cecil Square to the Broadstairs library of Nuckell, and the Ramsgate ball-room of the Albion Hotel! Captain C____ was a character! he valued himself on being the living picture of George IV.

Grand Assembly Room at Margate

CHAPTER THREE

PAGES FOR LEGENDS

RICHARD BARHAM

Another abundant contributor to literary magazines in the first half of the nineteenth century was **Richard Barham** (1788 - 1845), a minister of the Church of England who wrote under the pseudonym of Thomas Ingoldsby. His most popular production was *The Ingoldsby Legends*, stories in verse and prose recounting myths, legends and ghost stories from around this and other countries of Europe. First published in 1837, the stories were compiled into three books in 1840, 1842 and 1847 and the books remained widely read throughout the nineteenth and twentieth centuries, almost becoming embedded in the national consciousness through being referenced in works by any number of classic writers, from Henry James to Dorothy Sayers. In a novel by Anthony Powell, *The Military Philosophers*, they even figure as a bit of light reading relief for the protagonist, Nick Jenkins, who has been grappling with Proust's *In Search of Lost Time*. Significant additions to their content were the illustrations done by such leading artists as George Cruikshank, John Tenniel and Arthur Rackham.

Richard Barham

Barham suffered from poor health following two unfortunate accidents involving first a mail coach at the age of fourteen, in which he lost the use of his right arm, and later a gig, when he broke a leg. Born in Canterbury and later holding several Kent parish posts, he was particularly well acquainted with stories from around Kent. His ailing health led him to spend many sojourns in Margate taking the sea air and it is not surprising therefore that two of his legends concern Thanet. Both are in the form of poetry and the source of both, he says, is a Mr Simpkinson, who is described by him as an erudite friend, fellow visitor to Margate and a 'Life Governor' of the town's Sea Bathing Infirmary. Mr Simpkinson tells the first story, apparently from direct experience:

Misadventures at Margate: A Legend of Jarvis's Jetty

'Twas in Margate last July, I walk'd upon the pier,
I saw a little vulgar Boy—I said, 'What make you here?
The gloom upon your youthful cheek speaks anything but joy;'
Again I said, 'What make you here, you little vulgar Boy?'

He frown'd, that little vulgar Boy,– he deem'd I meant to scoff –
And when the little heart is big, a little 'sets it off;'
He put his finger in his mouth, his little bosom rose,–
He had no little handkerchief to wipe his little nose!

'Hark! don't you hear, my little man?– it's striking Nine,' I said,
'An hour when all good little boys and girls should be in bed.
Run home and get your supper, else your Ma' will scold—Oh! fie!
It's very wrong indeed for little boys to stand and cry!'

The tear-drop in his little eye again began to spring,
His bosom throbb'd with agony,– he cried like any thing!
I stoop'd, and thus amidst his sobs I heard him murmur –'Ah!
I haven't got no supper! and I haven't got no Ma'!!–

And I am here, on this here pier, to roam the world alone;
I have not had, this live-long day, one drop to cheer my heart,
Nor *"brown"* to buy a bit of bread with,– let alone a tart!

'If there's a soul will give me food, or find me in employ,
By day or night, then blow me tight!' (he was a vulgar Boy;)
'And now I'm here, from this here pier it is my fixed intent
To jump, as Mister Levi did from off the Monu-ment!'

'Cheer up! cheer up! my little man—cheer up!' I kindly said,
'You are a naughty boy to take such things into your head:
If you should jump from off the pier, you'd surely break your legs,
Perhaps your neck—then Bogey'd have you, sure as eggs are eggs!

'Come home with me, my little man, come home with me and sup;
My landlady is Mrs. Jones—we must not keep her up –
There's roast potatoes at the fire,– enough for me and you –
Come home you little vulgar Boy—I lodge at Number 2.'
I took him home to Number 2, the house beside 'The Foy,'
I bade him wipe his dirty shoes,– that little vulgar Boy,–
And then I said to Mistress Jones, the kindest of her sex,
'Pray be so good as go and fetch a pint of double X!'
But Mrs. Jones was rather cross, she made a little noise,
She said she 'did not like to wait on little vulgar Boys.'
She with her apron wiped the plates, and as she rubbed the delf,
Said I might 'go to Jericho, and fetch my beer myself!'
I did not go to Jericho—I went to Mr. Cobb –
I changed a shilling–(which in town the people call 'a Bob')–
It was not so much for myself as for that vulgar child–
And I said, 'A pint of double X, and please to draw it mild!'–

When I came back I gazed about—I gazed on stool and chair –
I could not see my little friend—because he was not there!
I peep'd beneath the table-cloth—beneath the sofa too –
I said, 'You little vulgar Boy! why what's become of you?'

I could not see my table-spoons—I look'd, but could not see
The little fiddle-pattern'd ones I use when I'm at tea;
– I could not see my sugar-tongs—my silver watch—oh, dear!
I know 'twas on the mantelpiece when I went out for beer.

I could not see my Macintosh—it was not to be seen!–
Nor yet my best white beaver hat, broad-brimm'd and lined with green;
My carpet-bag—my cruet-stand, that holds my sauce and soy,–
My roast potatoes!– all are gone!– and so's that vulgar Boy!

I rang the bell for Mrs. Jones, for she was down below,
'Oh, Mrs. Jones, what do you think?– ain't this a pretty go?–
– That horrid little vulgar Boy whom I brought here to-night,
– He's stolen my things and run away!!'– Says she, 'And sarve you right!!'

* * * * * * * * * * * * * *

Next morning I was up betimes—I sent the Crier round,
All with his bell and gold-laced hat to say I'd give a pound
To find that little vulgar Boy, who'd gone and used me so;
But when the Crier cried, 'O Yes!' the people cried, 'O No!'

I went to 'Jarvis' Landing-place,' the glory of the town,
There was a common sailor-man a-walking up and down,
I told my tale—he seem'd to think I'd not been treated well,
And call'd me 'Poor old Buffer!'– what that means I cannot tell.
That Sailor-man he said he'd seen that morning on the shore,
A son of—something –'twas a name I'd never heard before,
A little 'gallows-looking chap'–dear me; what could he mean?
With a 'carpet-swab' and 'muckingtogs,' and a hat turned up with green.

He spoke about his 'precious eyes,' and said he'd seen him 'sheer,'
– It's very odd that Sailor-men should talk so very queer –
And then he hitch'd his trousers up, as is, I'm told, their use,
– It's very odd that Sailor-men should wear those things so loose.

I did not understand him well, but think he meant to say
He'd seen that little vulgar Boy, that morning, swim away
In Captain Large's *Royal George*, about an hour before,
And they were now, as he supposed, 'somewheres' about the Nore.
A landsman said, 'I *twig* the chap—he's been upon the Mill –
And 'cause he *gammons* so the *flats*, ve calls him Veeping Bill!'

He said 'he'd done me wery brown,' and nicely '*stow'd* the *swag*,'
– That's French, I fancy, for a hat—or else a carpet-bag.
I went and told the constable my property to track;
He ask'd me if 'I did not wish that I might get it back?'

I answered, 'To be sure I do!– it's what I'm come about.'
He smiled and said, 'Sir, does your mother know that you are out?'
Not knowing what to do, I thought I'd hasten back to town,
And beg our own Lord Mayor to catch the Boy who'd 'done me brown.'

His Lordship very kindly said he'd try and find him out,
But he 'rather thought that there were several vulgar boys about.'
He sent for Mr. Withair then, and I described 'the swag,'
My Macintosh, my sugar-tongs, my spoons and carpet-bag;
He promised that the New Police should all their powers employ!
But never to this hour have I beheld that vulgar Boy!

Moral

Remember, then, that when a boy I've heard my Grandma tell,
'Be warn'd in time by others' harm, and you shall do full well!'
Don't link yourself with vulgar folks, who've got no fixed abode,
Tell lies, use naughty words, and say they 'wish they may be blow'd!'

Don't take too much of double X!– and don't at night go out
To fetch your beer yourself, but make the pot-boy bring your stout!
And when you go to Margate next, just stop, and ring the bell,
Give my respects to Mrs. Jones, and say I'm pretty well!

Notes
QUI FACIT PER ALIUM, FACIT PER SE—Deem not, gentle stranger, that Mr. Cobb is a petty dealer and chapman, as Mr. Simpkinson would here seem to imply. He is a maker, not a retailer of stingo,– and mighty pretty tipple he makes.

Blue plaque at 20 The Parade, Margate

This picture of Margate may still resonate today, but the 'Jarvis Jetty' of the story is, needless to say, long gone. The 1,100 foot wooden jetty called the 'Jarvis Landing Stage' was erected in 1824 by the Margate Pier Harbour Co. A charming gouache and watercolour painting of the jetty by Turner, done between 1829–40, which he entitles *Figures at Jarvis's Landing Place*, gives a good idea of what it was like. Subsequently the jetty was replaced in 1855 by the iron Margate Pier, better known as the Margate Jetty, which lived on until 1976 and is itself now long gone

Barham's second Thanet story takes us back to that perennial topic of local fascination, smuggling. Here we meet the useful Mr Simpkinson again, who relays the story he heard while at the Sea-Bathing Infirmary one day. As Barham writes: *"It is to my excellent and erudite friend, Simpkinson, that I am indebted for his graphic description of the well-known chalk-pit, between Acol and Minster, in the Isle of Thanet, known by the name of the 'Smuggler's Leap'."*

The story comes with an explanatory introduction, as follows:

THE SMUGGLER'S LEAP
A LEGEND OF THANET

Near this hamlet (Acol) is a long-disused chalk-pit of formidable depth, known by the name of "The Smuggler's Leap." The tradition of the parish runs, that a riding-officer from Sandwich, called Anthony Gill, lost his life here in the early part of the present (last) century, while in pursuit of a smuggler. A fog coming on, both parties went over the precipice. The smuggler's horse *only*, it is said, was found crushed beneath its rider. The spot has, of course, been haunted ever since.

The fire-flash shines from Reculver cliff,
And the answering light burns blue in the skiff,
And there they stand,
That smuggling band,
Some in the water and some on the sand,
Ready those contraband goods to land:
The night is dark, they are silent and still,
— At the head of the party is Smuggler Bill!

'Now lower away! come, lower away!
We must be far ere the dawn of the day.
If Exciseman Gill should get scent of the prey,
And should come, and should catch us here, what would he say?
Come, lower away, lads — once on the hill,
We'll laugh, ho! ho! at Exciseman Gill!'

The cargo's lower'd from the dark skiff's side,
And the tow-line drags the tubs through the tide,
No trick nor flam,
But your real Schiedam.
'Now mount, my merry men, mount and ride!'
Three on the crupper and one before,
And the led-horse laden with five tubs more;
But the rich point-lace,
In the oil-skin case
Of proof to guard its contents from ill,
The 'prime of the swag,' is with Smuggler Bill!

Merrily now in a goodly row,
Away and away those Smugglers go,
And they laugh at Exciseman Gill, ho! ho!
When out from the turn
Of the road to Herne,

Comes Gill, wide awake to the whole concern!
Exciseman Gill, in all his pride,
With his Custom-house officers all at his side!
— They were called Custom-house officers then;
There were no such things as 'Preventive men.'
Sauve qui peut!
That lawless crew,
Away, and away, and away they flew!
Some dropping one tub, some dropping two;–
Some gallop this way, and some gallop that,
Through Fordwich Level — o'er Sandwich Flat,

Some fly that way, and some fly this,
Like a covey of birds when the sportsmen miss;
These in their hurry
Make for Sturry,
With Custom-house officers close in their rear,
Down Rushbourne Lane, and so by Westbere,
None of them stopping,
But shooting and popping,
And many a Custom-house bullet goes slap
Through many a three-gallon tub like a tap,
And the gin spirts out
And squirts all about,
And many a heart grew sad that day
That so much good liquor was so thrown away.

Sauve qui peut! That lawless crew,
Away, and away, and away they flew!
Some seek Whitstable — some Grove Ferry,
Spurring and whipping like madmen — very —
For the life! for the life! they ride! they ride!
And the Custom-house officers all divide,

And they gallop on after them far and wide!
All, all, save one — Exciseman Gill,–
He sticks to the skirts of Smuggler Bill!

Smuggler Bill is six feet high,
He has curling locks, and a roving eye,
He has a tongue and he has a smile
Trained the female heart to beguile,
And there is not a farmer's wife in the Isle,
From St. Nicholas quite
To the Foreland Light,
But that eye, and that tongue, and that smile will wheedle her
To have done with the Grocer and make him her Tea-dealer;
There is not a farmer there but he still
Buys gin and tobacco from Smuggler Bill.

Smuggler Bill rides gallant and gay
On his dapple-grey mare, away, and away,
And he pats her neck and he seems to say,
'Follow who will, ride after who may,
In sooth he had need
Fodder his steed,
In lieu of Lent-corn, with a Quicksilver feed;
— Nor oats, nor beans, nor the best of old hay,
Will make him a match for my own dapple-grey!
Ho! ho!– ho! ho!' says Smuggler Bill —
He draws out a flask and he sips his fill,
And he laughs 'Ho! ho!' at Exciseman Gill.
Down Chislett Lane, so free and so fleet
Rides Smuggler Bill, and away to Up-street;
Sarre Bridge is won —
Bill thinks it fun;
'Ho! ho! the old tub-gauging son of a gun —

His wind will be thick, and his breeks be thin,
Ere a race like this he may hope to win!'

Away, away
Goes the fleet dapple-grey,
Fresh as the breeze and free as the wind,
And Exciseman Gill lags far behind.
'I would give my soul,' quoth Exciseman Gill,
'For a nag that would catch that Smuggler Bill!–
No matter for blood, no matter for bone,
No matter for colour, bay, brown or roan,
So I had but one!' A voice cried 'Done!'
'Ay, dun,' said Exciseman Gill, and he spied
A Custom-house officer close by his side,
On a high-trotting horse with a dun-coloured hide.–
'Devil take me,' again quoth Exciseman Gill,
'If I had but that horse, I'd have Smuggler Bill!'

From his using such shocking expressions, it's plain
That Exciseman Gill was rather profane.
He was, it is true,
As bad as a Jew,
A sad old scoundrel as ever you knew,
And he rode in his stirrups sixteen stone two.
— He'd just utter'd the words which I've mention'd to you,
When his horse coming slap on his knees with him, threw
Him head over heels, and away he flew,
And Exciseman Gill was bruised black and blue.

When he arose
His hands and his clothes
Were as filthy as could be,– he'd pitch'd on his nose,

And roll'd over and over again in the mud,
And his nose and his chin were all cover'd with blood;
Yet he screamed with passion, 'I'd rather grill
Than not come up with that Smuggler Bill!'
–'Mount! Mount!' quoth the Custom-house officer, 'get
On the back of my Dun, you'll bother him yet.
Your words are plain, though they're somewhat rough,
'Done and Done' between gentlemen's always enough!–
I'll lend you a lift — there — you're up on him — so,
He's a rum one to look at — a devil to go!'
Exciseman Gill
Dash'd up the hill,
And mark'd not, so eager was he in pursuit,
The queer Custom-house officer's queer-looking boot.
Smuggler Bill rides on amain,
He slacks not girth and he draws not rein,
Yet the dapple-grey mare bounds on in vain,
For nearer now — and he hears it plain —
Sounds the tramp of a horse –'Tis the Gauger again!'
Smuggler Bill
Dashes round by the mill
That stands near the road upon Monkton Hill,–
'Now speed,– now speed,
My dapple-grey steed,
Thou ever, my dapple, wert good at need!
O'er Monkton Mead, and through Minster Level,
We'll baffle him yet, be he gauger or devil!
For Manston Cave, away! away!
Now speed thee, now speed thee, my good dapple-grey,
It shall never be said that Smuggler Bill
Was run down like a hare by Exciseman Gill!'

Manston Cave was Bill's abode;
A mile to the north of the Ramsgate road.
(Of late they say
It's been taken away,
That is, levell'd and filled up with chalk and clay,
By a gentleman there of the name of Day,)
Thither he urges his good dapple-grey;
And the dapple-grey steed,
Still good at need,
Though her chest it pants, and her flanks they bleed,
Dashes along at the top of her speed;
But nearer and nearer Exciseman Gill
Cries 'Yield thee! now yield thee, thou Smuggler Bill!'

Smuggler Bill, he looks behind,
And he sees a Dun horse come swift as the wind,
And his nostrils smoke and his eyes they blaze
Like a couple of lamps on a yellow post-chaise!
Every shoe he has got
Appears red-hot!
And sparks round his ears snap, crackle, and play,
And his tail cocks up in a very odd way;
Every hair in his mane seems a porcupine's quill,
And there on his back sits Exciseman Gill,
Crying 'Yield thee! now yield thee, thou Smuggler Bill!'
Smuggler Bill from his holster drew
A large horse-pistol, of which he had two!
Made by Nock;
He pull'd back the cock
As far as he could to the back of the lock;
The trigger he touch'd, and the welkin rang
To the sound of the weapon, it made such a bang;

Smuggler Bill ne'er missed his aim,
The shot told true on the Dun — but there came
From the hole where it enter'd — not blood,– but flame,
— He changed his plan,
And fired at the man;
But his second horse-pistol flashed in the pan!
And Exciseman Gill with a hearty good will,
Made a grab at the collar of Smuggler Bill.

The dapple-grey mare made a desperate bound
When that queer Dun horse on her flank she found,
Alack! and alas! on what dangerous ground!
It's enough to make one's flesh to creep
To stand on that fearful verge, and peep
Down the rugged sides so dreadfully steep,
Where the chalk-hole yawns full sixty feet deep,
O'er which that steed took that desperate leap!
It was so dark then under the trees,
No horse in the world could tell chalk from cheese —
Down they went — o'er that terrible fall,–
Horses, Exciseman, Smuggler, and all!!

Below were found
Next day on the ground
By an elderly Gentleman walking his round,
(I wouldn't have seen such a sight for a pound,)
All smash'd and dash'd, three mangled corses,
Two of them human,– the third was a horse's —
That good dapple-grey, and Exciseman Gill
Yet grasping the collar of Smuggler Bill!
But where was the Dun? that terrible Dun?
From that terrible night he was seen by none!–
There are some people think, though I am not one,

That part of the story all nonsense and fun,
But the country-folks there,
One and all declare,
When the 'Crowner's 'Quest' came to sit on the pair,
They heard a loud Horse-laugh up in the air!–
— If in one of the trips
Of the steam-boat Eclipse
You should go down to Margate to look at the ships,
Or to take what the bathing-room people call 'Dips,'
You may hear old folks talk
Of that quarry of chalk:
Or go over — it's rather too far for a walk,
But a three-shilling drive will give you a peep
At that fearful chalk-pit — so awfully deep,
Which is call'd to this moment 'The Smuggler's Leap!'
Nay more, I am told, on a moonshiny night,
If you're 'plucky,' and not over subject to fright,
And go and look over that chalk-pit white,
You may see, if you will,
The Ghost of Old Gill
Grappling the Ghost of Smuggler Bill,
And the Ghost of the dapple-grey lying between 'em.–
I'm told so — I can't say I know one who's seen 'em!

MORAL.
And now, gentle Reader, one word ere we part,
Just take a friend's counsel, and lay it to heart.
Imprimis, don't smuggle!– if bent to please Beauty
You must buy French lace,– purchase what has paid duty
Don't use naughty words, in the next place,– and ne'er in
Your language adopt a bad habit of swearing!
Never say 'Devil take me!'

> Or 'shake me!'–or 'bake me!'
> Or such-like expressions — Remember Old Nick
> To take folks at their word is remarkably quick.
> Another sound maxim I'd wish you to keep,
> Is, 'Mind what you're after, and — Look ere you Leap!'
> Above all, to my last gravest caution attend —
> *NEVER BORROW A HORSE YOU DON'T KNOW OF A FRIEND!!!*

In his capacity as a church minister, Barham was no doubt unable to resist the need to conclude his stories with a moral, adding a dash of spice and tongue-in-cheek admonishment to his poetic narrative.

As to the actual location of the chalk-pit of the 'Smuggler's Leap' story, we read in a book by Charles Harper published in 1904 called *The Ingoldsby Country* the following description:

The chalk-pit, too is sufficiently real. Crossing the open fields, spread starkly to the sky, between Monkton and Cleve Court, it is found on the Ramsgate road, opposite the "Prospect" Inn, where it still gapes as deep and wide as ever. Do not, however, if you wish to be impressed with the truth of Ingoldsby's romantic description, view it by the brilliant sunlight of a summer's day, because at such times the great cleft in the dull white of the chalk does not properly proclaim its immensity. It is only when the evening shadows fall obliquely into the old chalk-pit that you applaud the spirit of those lines:

> It's enough to make one's flesh to creep
> To stand on that fearful verge, and peep
> Down the rugged sides so dreadfully steep,
> Where the chalk-hole yawns full sixty feet deep.

Today the legend is commemorated somewhat differently. Unlikely though it may seem, a park containing retirement homes, called 'Smuggler's Leap Residential Park', has been created in the very same chalk-pit, at the A299 roundabout leading to Minster. Fortunately no reports of ghosts have been reported by residents, in spite of the claim that the spot has been haunted ever since. Perhaps, after all, the spirits of Gill and Bill have found some comfort in the park, and themselves gone into retirement there.

Smuggler's Leap Residential Park

CHAPTER FOUR

POETIC PAGES

SAMUEL TAYLOR COLERIDGE

Tempering the qualities of frivolity and sexual ardour, so alarming to Jane Austen, with poetic genius and huge intellect, **Samuel Taylor Coleridge** (1772 – 1834) was the greatest early nineteenth century advocate of the charms of Ramsgate. He loved the place and even coined the word 'Ramsgatize' to describe the extended visits he made to the seaside town almost every year from 1819 to his death in 1834. The strange *ménage ã trois* that he had fallen into at his lodgings in Highgate, London, continued in Ramsgate when he accompanied the couple he lived with, James and Anne Gillman, on their holidays to the Thanet town. Sometimes he came only with Anne when James was unable to get away from London.

Samuel Taylor Coleridge

Coleridge's great pastime at the seaside, apart from a very active social round and philosophical or literary discussion, was swimming. He was frequently down on one of the beaches heading into the water, come rain or shine, and however cold the weather, even in November. So it is no surprise that he gives us little pictures of Ramsgate in some of his poems. In his wistful poem *Youth and Age*, which he started writing in 1823, we get a tiny glimpse of the cliffs and sands of Ramsgate that he loved so much, highlighted in the poem below. They are not specifically named in the poem, but there can be little doubt that they refer to the cliffs and sands at Ramsgate. Furthermore, he seems to make a reference to the new steam powered boats that were very popular in his time, and perhaps by inference to the new paddle-steamers that he well knew and which took passengers from London to Margate and Ramsgate, rendering them poetically and even fondly as ' those trim skiffs, unknown of yore… that ask no aid of sail or oar'. He had none of the reservations of Charles Lamb here, who disliked the belching smoke of the machine age and preferred the simple sails of the 'hoy'. Perhaps Coleridge was even prefiguring Turner, who artistically rendered steam and paddle in his famous painting of 1839, *The Fighting Temeraire*, where the tug is a paddle boat. Coleridge's finely wrought poem is such an evocative addition to the 'youth goes over' *genre* that it is quoted here in full, and was reputedly one of Coleridge's favourites:

Youth and Age

Verse, a breeze mid blossoms straying,
Where Hope clung feeding, like a bee—
Both were mine! Life went a-maying
With Nature, Hope, and Poesy,
When I was young!
When I was young?—Ah, woful When!
Ah! for the change 'twixt Now and Then!
This breathing house not built with hands,
This body that does me grievous wrong,
O'er aery cliffs and glittering sands,
How lightly then it flashed along:—
Like those trim skiffs, unknown of yore,
On winding lakes and rivers wide,
That ask no aid of sail or oar,
That fear no spite of wind or tide!
Nought cared this body for wind or weather
When Youth and I lived in't together.
Flowers are lovely; Love is flower-like;
Friendship is a sheltering tree;

O! the joys, that came down shower-like,
Of Friendship, Love, and Liberty,
Ere I was old!
Ere I was old? Ah woful Ere,
Which tells me, Youth's no longer here!
O Youth! for years so many and sweet,
'Tis known, that Thou and I were one,
I'll think it but a fond conceit—
It cannot be that Thou art gone!
Thy vesper-bell hath not yet toll'd:—
And thou wert aye a masker bold!
What strange disguise hast now put on,
To make believe, that thou are gone?
I see these locks in silvery slips,
This drooping gait, this altered size:
But Spring-tide blossoms on thy lips,
And tears take sunshine from thine eyes!
Life is but thought: so think I will
That Youth and I are house-mates still.
But the tears of mournful eve!
Where no hope is, life's a warning
That only serves to make us grieve,
When we are old:
That only serves to make us grieve
With oft and tedious taking-leave,
Like some poor nigh-related guest,
That may not rudely be dismist;
Yet hath outstay'd his welcome while,
And tells the jest without the smile.

An early 19th century paddle steamer leaving Ramsgate Harbour: with some additional 'aid of sail'

Coleridge is more explicit in his reference to Ramsgate and to the coast bordering Broadstairs in his poem *The Delinquent Travellers*. This poem of 1824 clearly owes its writing to his stays Ramsgate, with the French coast opposite in view and in mind. As he lambasts the restless and misguided travellers who must always be off visiting some foreign land while 'he cannot go' and must stay (striking a chord in our Covid age), he specifically mentions and names Dumpton Bay, the bay between Ramsgate and Broadstairs. He also cannot resist alluding to the perennial topic of smuggling in the area, and shows he was well aware that Dumpton Gap was a favourite rendezvous for a smuggling run. This amusingly barbed poem is printed in full, with the section referring both to Ramsgate and to the infamous Thanet smugglers highlighted in bold:

The Delinquent Travellers

Some are home-sick—some two or three;
Their third year on the Arctic Sea--
Brave Captain Lyon tells us so--
Spite of those charming Esquimaux,
But O, what scores are sick of Home,
Agog for Paris or for Rome!

Nay! tho' contented to abide,
You should prefer your own fireside;
Yet since grim War has ceased its madding,

And Peace has set John Bull agadding,
'Twould such a vulgar taste betray,
For very shame you must away!
"What? not yet seen the coast of France!
The folks will swear, for lack of bail,
You've spent your last five years in jail!'
Keep moving! Steam, or Gas, or Stage,
Hold, cabin, steerage, hencoop's cage--
Tour, Journey, Voyage, Lounge, Ride, Walk,
Skim, Sketch, Excursion, Travel-talk--
For move you must! 'Tis now the rage,
The law and fashion of the Age.
If you but perch, where Dover tallies,
So strangely with the coast of Calais,
With a good glass and knowing look,
You'll soon get matter for a book!
Or else, in Gas-car, take your chance
Like that adventurous king of France,
Who, once, with twenty thousand men
Went up--and then came down again;
At least, he moved if nothing more:
And if there's nought left to explore,
Yet while your well-greased wheels keep spinning,
The traveller's honoured name you're winning,
And, snug as Jonas in the Whale,
You may loll back and dream a tale.
Move, or be moved--there's no protection,
Our Mother Earth has ta'en the infection--
(That rogue Copernicus, 'tis said
First put the whirring in her head),
A planet She, and can't endure
T'exist without her annual Tour:

The name were else a mere misnomer,
Since Planet is but Greek for Roamer.
The atmosphere, too, can do no less
Than ventilate her emptiness,
Bilks turn-pike gates, for no one cares,
And gives herself a thousand airs--
While streams and shopkeepers, we see,
Will have their run toward the sea--
And if, meantime, like old King Log,
Or ass with tether and a clog,
Must graze at home! to yawn and bray
"I guess we shall have rain to-day!'
Nor clog nor tether can be worse
Than the dead palsy of the purse.
Money, I've heard a wise man say,
Makes herself wings and flies away:
Ah! would She take it in her head
To make a pair for me instead!
At all events, the Fancy's free,
No traveller so bold as she.
From Fear and Poverty released
I'll saddle Pegasus, at least,
And when she's seated to her mind,
I within I can mount behind:
And since this outward I, you know,
Must stay because he cannot go,
My fellow-travellers shall be they
Who go because they cannot stay--
Rogues, rascals, sharpers, blanks and prizes,
Delinquents of all sorts and sizes,
Fraudulent bankrupts, Knights burglarious,
And demireps of means precarious--
All whom Law thwarted, Arms or Arts,

Compel to visit foreign parts,
All hail! No compliments, I pray,
I'll follow where you lead the way!
But ere we cross the main once more,
Methinks, along my native shore,
Dismounting from my steed I'll stray
Beneath the cliffs of Dumpton Bay,
Where, Ramsgate and Broadstairs between,
Rude caves and grated doors are seen:
And here I'll watch till break of day,
(For Fancy in her magic might
Can turn broad noon to starless night!)
When lo! methinks a sudden band
Of smock-clad smugglers round me stand.
Denials, oaths, in vain I try,
At once they gag me for a spy.
And stow me in the boat hard by.
Suppose us fairly now afloat,
Till Boulogne mouth receives our Boat.
But, bless us! what a numerous band
Of cockneys anglicize the strand!
Delinquent bankrupts, leg-bailed debtors,
Some for the news, and some for letters--
With hungry look and tarnished dress,
French shrugs and British surliness.
Sick of the country for their sake
Of them and France French leave I take--
And lo! a transport comes in view
I hear the merry motley crew,
Well skilled in pocket to make entry,
Of Dieman's Land the elected Gentry,
And founders of Australian Races.--
The Rogues! I see it in their faces!
Receive me, Lads! I'll go with you,
Hunt the black swan and kangaroo,

And that New Holland we'll presume
Old England with some elbow-room.
Across the mountains we will roam,
And each man make himself a home:
Or, if old habits ne'er forsaking,
Like clock-work of the Devil's making,
Ourselves inveterate rogues should be,
We'll have a virtuous progeny;
And on the dunghill of our vices
Raise human pine-apples and spices.
Of all the children of John Bull
With empty heads and bellies full,
Who ramble East, West, North and South,
With leaky purse and open mouth,
In search of varieties exotic
The usefullest and most patriotic,
And merriest, too, believe me, Sirs!
Are your Delinquent Travellers!

Dumpton Bay, with Ramsgate's 'aery cliffs and glittering sands' stretching beyond

CHAPTER FIVE

THE ISLE OF DICKENS

CHARLES DICKENS

No writer made the Isle of Thanet more his own than **Charles Dickens** (1812 – 1870). For him the isle was a great discovery: a place of escape from the metropolis where he could write in peace, and a wild, woolly, out-of-the-way, eccentric place, full of characters, that suited his creative temperament. 'This forlorn Isle of Thanet – *Cette Ile désolée de Thanet*', as he said to Count D'Orsay, one of his many French literary friends, perhaps gazing at the coast opposite and thinking of his frequent trips across the channel, 'I love it all the same because it is quiet and I can think and dream here, like a giant – *Je l'aime néanmoins parce qu'elle est tranquille et je puis penser et rêver ici, comme un géant.*'

Charles Dickens

Dickens' acquaintance with Thanet first started in the early 1800s, as clearly shown through his using Ramsgate as the setting for one of his short stories. This story, *The Tuggses at Ramsgate*, forms part of Dickens' first venture into fiction when he wrote under the pseudonym Boz, and appeared as one of his *Sketches by Boz - Illustrative of Every-day Live and Every-day People*. The sketches appeared in various newspapers and periodicals between 1833–36 and gave ample indication of Dickens' incipient genius for writing. *The Tuggses at Ramsgate*, which was published in the *The Library of Fiction*, is no exception here, and is an amusing and beautifully constructed story of show-off *nouveaux riches* from London getting their comeuppance. The Tuggs family come into a windfall of £20,000 and elevate themselves from chandler-class to monied-class, deciding to spend the summer season in Ramsgate. Unfortunately, while they are on the boat to Ramsgate, a couple practised in the art of confidence tricks, Captain Walter Waters and his wife Belinda, spot them in their attempts to rise socially, play on their aspirations, with the wife deceiving the son Simon (who has gentrified his name to the more culturally resonant Cymon) into believing she is in love with him. A compromising situation is engineered by the cunning pair resulting in the Tuggses finding themselves £1,500 lighter after being forced into a settlement to hush things up.

Here is one of Dickens' pictures of Ramsgate from the story:

From *The Tuggses at Ramsgate* (1836):

If the pier had presented a scene of life and bustle to the Tuggses on their first landing at Ramsgate, it was far surpassed by the appearance of the sands on the morning after their arrival. It was a fine, bright, clear day, with a light breeze from the sea. There were the same ladies and gentlemen, the same children, the same nursemaids, the same telescopes, the same portable chairs. The ladies were employed in needlework, or watch-guard making, or knitting, or reading novels; the gentlemen were reading newspapers and magazines; the children were digging holes in the sand with wooden spades, and collecting water therein; the nursemaids, with their youngest charges in their arms, were running in after the waves, and then running back with the waves after them; and, now and then, a little sailing-boat either departed with a gay and talkative cargo of passengers, or returned with a very silent and particularly uncomfortable-looking one.

'Well, I never!' exclaimed Mrs. Tuggs, as she and Mr. Joseph Tuggs, and Miss Charlotta Tuggs, and Mr. Cymon Tuggs, with their eight feet in a corresponding number of yellow shoes, seated themselves on four rush-bottomed chairs, which, being placed in a soft part of the sand, forthwith sunk down some two feet and a half—'Well, I never!'

Mr. Cymon, by an exertion of great personal strength, uprooted the chairs, and removed them further back.

'Why, I'm blessed if there ain't some ladies a-going in!' exclaimed Mr. Joseph Tuggs, with intense astonishment.

'Lor, pa!' exclaimed Miss Charlotta.

'There is, my dear,' said Mr. Joseph Tuggs. And, sure enough, four young ladies, each furnished with a towel, tripped up the steps of a bathing-machine. In went the horse, floundering about in the water; round turned the machine; down sat the driver; and presently out burst the young ladies aforesaid, with four distinct splashes.

'Well, that's sing'ler, too!' ejaculated Mr. Joseph Tuggs, after an awkward pause. Mr. Cymon coughed slightly.

'Why, here's some gentlemen a-going in on this side!' exclaimed Mrs. Tuggs, in a tone of horror.

Three machines—three horses—three flounderings—three turnings round—three splashes—three gentlemen, disporting themselves in the water like so many dolphins.

'Well, that's sing'ler!' said Mr. Joseph Tuggs again. Miss Charlotta coughed this time, and another pause ensued. It was agreeably broken.

'How d'ye do, dear? We have been looking for you, all the morning,' said a voice to Miss Charlotta Tuggs. Mrs. Captain Waters was the owner of it.

'How d'ye do?' said Captain Walter Waters, all suavity; and a most cordial interchange of greetings ensued.

'Belinda, my love,' said Captain Walter Waters, applying his glass to his eye, and looking in the direction of the sea.

'Yes, my dear,' replied Mrs. Captain Waters.

'There's Harry Thompson!'

'Where?' said Belinda, applying her glass to her eye.

'Bathing.'

'Lor, so it is! He don't see us, does he?'

'No, I don't think he does' replied the captain. 'Bless my soul, how very singular!'

'What?' inquired Belinda.

'There's Mary Golding, too.'

'Lor!—where?' (Up went the glass again.)

'There!' said the captain, pointing to one of the young ladies before noticed, who, in her bathing costume, looked as if she was enveloped in a patent Mackintosh, of scanty dimensions.

'So it is, I declare!' exclaimed Mrs. Captain Waters. 'How very curious we should see them both!'

'Very,' said the captain, with perfect coolness.

'It's the reg'lar thing here, you see,' whispered Mr. Cymon Tuggs to his father.

'I see it is,' whispered Mr. Joseph Tuggs in reply. 'Queer, though—ain't it?' Mr. Cymon Tuggs nodded assent.

'What do you think of doing with yourself this morning?' inquired the captain. 'Shall we lunch at Pegwell?'

'I should like that very much indeed,' interposed Mrs. Tuggs. She had never heard of Pegwell; but the word 'lunch' had reached her ears, and it sounded very agreeably.

But while Ramsgate provided the stepping stone for Dickens into Thanet, it was Broadstairs that became his home from home. He came to Broadstairs in 1837 to finish *The Pickwick Papers*, renting rooms at the top of the High Street, and spent the early to late summer months in the town almost every year for the next fifteen years, mixing work with a little holiday. As Broadstairs was such a special place for him, it was inevitable that local scenes should work their way into his writing. It was while looking out to the storm-tossed sea and the dangerous Goodwin Sands from his study in Fort House (later re-named Bleak House after his death) that he wrote the famous storm and shipwreck scene in *David Copperfield*, in which David's friend Steerforth dies, and which he transposes to Yarmouth in the novel. Similarly, the home of David Copperfield's aunt, Betsy Trotwood, in spite of being located in Dover in the novel, was in reality based on a house on Broadstairs sea front, now known as Dickens House, whose owner, Miss Mary Pearson Strong, was the precise model of Miss Betsey Trotwood.

Dickens was often invited in for tea with Miss Strong and so had no difficulty in transferring his impressions of her distinctive parlour to his evocation of Betsey Trotwood's parlour in the novel. He also wickedly makes use of the real-life Miss Strong's almost manic reaction to the donkeys and their riders that rashly ventured on to the grass in front of her house. Both the house and 'the little piece of green in front' are still there to this day, with the house now converted into a Dickens museum and the parlour recreated and filled with objects just as described in the novel:

From *David Copperfield* (1850):

As I laid down my pen, a moment since, to think of it, the air from the sea came blowing in again, mixed with the perfume of the flowers; and I saw the old-fashioned furniture brightly rubbed and polished, my aunt's inviolable chair and table by the round green fan in the bow-window, the drugget-covered carpet, the cat, the kettle-holder, the two canaries, the old china, the punchbowl full of dried rose-leaves, the tall press guarding all sorts of bottles and pots, and, wonderfully out of keeping with the rest, my dusty self upon the sofa, taking note of everything.

Janet had gone away to get the bath ready, when my aunt, to my great alarm, became in one moment rigid with indignation, and had hardly voice to cry out, 'Janet! Donkeys!'

Upon which, Janet came running up the stairs as if the house were in flames, darted out on a little piece of green in front, and warned off two saddle-donkeys, lady-ridden, that had presumed to set hoof upon it; while my aunt, rushing out of the house, seized the bridle of a third animal laden with a bestriding child, turned him, led him forth from those sacred precincts, and boxed the ears of the unlucky urchin in attendance who had dared to profane that hallowed ground.

To this hour I don't know whether my aunt had any lawful right of way over that patch of green; but she had settled it in her own mind that she had, and it was all the same to her. The one great outrage of her life, demanding to be constantly avenged, was the passage of a donkey over that immaculate spot. In whatever occupation she was engaged, however interesting to her the conversation in which she was taking part, a donkey turned the current of her ideas in a moment, and she was upon him straight. Jugs of water, and watering-pots, were kept in secret places ready to be discharged on the offending boys; sticks were laid in ambush behind the door; sallies were made at all hours; and incessant war prevailed. Perhaps this was an agreeable excitement to the donkey-boys; or perhaps the more sagacious of the donkeys, understanding how the case stood, delighted with constitutional obstinacy in coming that way. I only know that there were three alarms before the bath was ready; and that on the occasion of the last and most desperate of all, I saw my aunt engage, single-handed, with a sandy-headed lad of fifteen, and bump his sandy head against her own gate, before he seemed to comprehend what was the matter. These interruptions were of the more ridiculous to me, because she was giving me broth out of a table-spoon at the time (having firmly persuaded herself that I was actually starving, and must receive nourishment at first in very small quantities), and, while my mouth was yet open to receive the spoon, she would put it back into the basin, cry 'Janet! Donkeys!' and go out to the assault.

Home of Miss Mary Pearson Strong, the original of Betsey Trotwood

In the end, after spending so much time in Broadstairs, Dickens could not resist composing a full-length portrait of the town rather than using the locality as an incidental inspiration and adjunct to his writing. So, as his swan-song in 1851, when he was about to exchange Broadstairs for Boulogne for his annual escape, he produced this richly comic, brilliantly observed and, in parts, gently mischievous piece, which he called *Our English Watering Place*, printed here in full.

Our English Watering-Place (1851):

IN the Autumn-time of the year, when the great metropolis is so much hotter, so much noisier, so much more dusty or so much more water-carted, so much more crowded, so much more disturbing and distracting in all respects, than it usually is, a quiet sea-beach becomes indeed a blessed spot. Half awake and half asleep, this idle morning in our sunny window on the edge of a chalk-cliff in the old-fashioned watering-place to which we are a faithful resorter, we feel a lazy inclination to sketch its picture.

The place seems to respond. Sky, sea, beach, and village, lie as still before us as if they were sitting for the picture. It is dead low-water. A ripple plays among the ripening corn upon the cliff, as if it were faintly trying from recollection to imitate the sea; and the world of butterflies hovering over the crop of radish-seed are as restless in their little way as the gulls are in their larger manner when the wind blows. But the ocean lies winking in the sunlight like a drowsy lion - its glassy waters scarcely curve upon the shore - the fishing-boats in the tiny harbour are all stranded in the mud - our two colliers (our watering-place has a maritime trade employing that amount of shipping) have not an inch of water within a quarter of a mile of them, and turn, exhausted, on their sides, like faint fish of an antediluvian species. Rusty cables and chains, ropes and rings, undermost parts of posts and piles and confused timber-defences against the waves, lie strewn about, in a brown litter of tangled sea-weed and fallen cliff which looks as if a family of giants had been making tea here for ages, and had observed an untidy custom of throwing their tea-leaves on the shore.

In truth, our watering-place itself has been left somewhat high and dry by the tide of years. Concerned as we are for its honour, we must reluctantly admit that the time when this pretty little semicircular sweep of houses, tapering off at the end of the wooden pier into a point in the sea, was a gay place, and when the lighthouse overlooking it shone at daybreak on company dispersing from public balls, is but dimly traditional now. There is a bleak chamber in our watering-place which is yet called the Assembly 'Rooms,' and understood to be available on hire for balls or concerts; and, some few seasons since, an ancient little gentleman came down and stayed at the hotel, who said that he had danced there, in bygone ages, with the Honourable Miss Peepy, well known to have been the Beauty of her day and the cruel occasion of innumerable duels. But he was so old and shrivelled, and so very rheumatic in the legs, that it demanded more imagination than our watering-place can usually muster, to believe him; therefore, except the Master of the 'Rooms' (who to this hour wears knee- breeches, and who confirmed the statement with tears in his eyes), nobody did believe in the little lame old gentleman, or even in the Honourable Miss Peepy, long deceased.

As to subscription balls in the Assembly Rooms of our watering- place now, red-hot cannon balls are less improbable. Sometimes, a misguided wanderer of a Ventriloquist, or an Infant Phenomenon, or a juggler, or somebody with an Orrery that is several stars behind the time, takes the place for a night, and issues bills with the name of his last town lined out, and the name of ours ignominiously written in, but you may be sure this never happens twice to the same unfortunate person. On such occasions the discoloured old Billiard Table that is seldom played at (unless the ghost of the Honourable Miss Peepy plays at pool with other ghosts) is pushed into a corner, and benches are solemnly constituted into front seats, back seats, and reserved seats - which are much the same after you have paid - and a few dull candles are lighted - wind permitting - and the performer and the scanty audience play out a short match which shall make the other most low-spirited - which is usually a drawn game. After that, the performer instantly departs with maledictory expressions, and is never heard of more.

But the most wonderful feature of our Assembly Rooms, is, that an annual sale of 'Fancy and other China,' is announced here with mysterious constancy and perseverance. Where the china comes from, where it goes to, why it is annually put up to auction when nobody ever thinks of bidding for it, how it comes to pass that it is always the same china, whether it would not have been cheaper, with the sea at hand, to have thrown it away, say in eighteen hundred and thirty, are standing enigmas. Every year the bills come out, every year the Master of the Rooms gets into a little pulpit on a table, and offers it for sale, every year nobody buys it, every year it is put away somewhere till next year, when it appears again as if the whole thing were a new idea. We have a faint remembrance of an unearthly collection of clocks, purporting to be the work of Parisian and Genevese artists - chiefly bilious-faced clocks, supported on sickly white crutches, with their pendulums dangling like lame legs - to which a similar course of events occurred for several years, until they seemed to lapse away, of mere imbecility.

Attached to our Assembly Rooms is a library. There is a wheel of fortune in it, but it is rusty and dusty, and never turns. A large doll, with moveable eyes, was put up to be raffled for, by five-and-twenty members at two shillings, seven years ago this autumn, and the list is not full yet. We are rather sanguine, now, that the raffle will come off next year. We think so, because we only want nine members, and should only want eight, but for number two having grown up since her name was entered, and withdrawn it when she was married. Down the street, there is a toy-ship of considerable burden, in the same condition. Two of the boys who were entered for that raffle have gone to India in real ships, since; and one was shot, and died in the arms of his sister's lover, by whom he sent his last words home.

This is the library for the Minerva Press. If you want that kind of reading, come to our watering-place. The leaves of the romances, reduced to a condition very like curl-paper, are thickly studded with notes in pencil: sometimes complimentary, sometimes jocose. Some of these commentators, like commentators in a more extensive way, quarrel with one another. One young gentleman who sarcastically writes 'O!!!' after every sentimental passage, is pursued through his literary career by another, who writes 'Insulting Beast!' Miss Julia Mills has read the whole collection of these books. She has left marginal notes on the pages, as 'Is not this truly touching? J. M.' 'How thrilling! J. M.' 'Entranced here by the Magician's potent spell. J. M.' She has also italicised her favourite traits in the description of the hero, as 'his hair, which was DARK and WAVY, clustered in RICH PROFUSION around a MARBLE BROW, whose lofty paleness bespoke the intellect within.' It reminds her of another hero. She adds, 'How like B. L. Can this be mere coincidence? J. M.'

You would hardly guess which is the main street of our watering- place, but you may know it by its being always stopped up with donkey-chaises. Whenever you come here, and see harnessed donkeys eating clover out of barrows drawn completely across a narrow thoroughfare, you may be quite sure you are in our High Street. Our Police you may know by his uniform, likewise by his never on any account interfering with anybody - especially the tramps and vagabonds. In our fancy shops we have a capital collection of damaged goods, among which the flies of countless summers 'have been roaming.' We are great in obsolete seals, and in faded pin- cushions, and in rickety camp-stools, and in exploded cutlery, and in miniature vessels, and in stunted little telescopes, and in objects made of shells that pretend not to be shells. Diminutive spades, barrows, and baskets, are our principal articles of commerce; but even they don't look quite new somehow. They always seem to have been offered and refused somewhere else, before they came down to our watering-place.

Yet, it must not be supposed that our watering-place is an empty place, deserted by all visitors except a few staunch persons of approved fidelity. On the contrary, the chances are that if you came down here in August or

September, you wouldn't find a house to lay your head in. As to finding either house or lodging of which you could reduce the terms, you could scarcely engage in a more hopeless pursuit. For all this, you are to observe that every season is the worst season ever known, and that the householding population of our watering-place are ruined regularly every autumn. They are like the farmers, in regard that it is surprising how much ruin they will bear. We have an excellent hotel - capital baths, warm, cold, and shower - first-rate bathing-machines - and as good butchers, bakers, and grocers, as heart could desire. They all do business, it is to be presumed, from motives of philanthropy - but it is quite certain that they are all being ruined. Their interest in strangers, and their politeness under ruin, bespeak their amiable nature. You would say so, if you only saw the baker helping a new comer to find suitable apartments.

So far from being at a discount as to company, we are in fact what would be popularly called rather a nobby place. Some tip-top 'Nobbs' come down occasionally - even Dukes and Duchesses. We have known such carriages to blaze among the donkey-chaises, as made beholders wink. Attendant on these equipages come resplendent creatures in plush and powder, who are sure to be stricken disgusted with the indifferent accommodation of our watering-place, and who, of an evening (particularly when it rains), may be seen very much out of drawing, in rooms far too small for their fine figures, looking discontentedly out of little back windows into bye-streets. The lords and ladies get on well enough and quite good-humouredly: but if you want to see the gorgeous phenomena who wait upon them at a perfect non-plus, you should come and look at the resplendent creatures with little back parlours for servants' halls, and turn-up bedsteads to sleep in, at our watering-place. You have no idea how they take it to heart.

We have a pier - a queer old wooden pier, fortunately without the slightest pretensions to architecture, and very picturesque in consequence. Boats are hauled up upon it, ropes are coiled all over it; lobster-pots, nets, masts, oars, spars, sails, ballast, and rickety capstans, make a perfect labyrinth of it. For ever hovering about this pier, with their hands in their pockets, or leaning over the rough bulwark it opposes to the sea, gazing through telescopes which they carry about in the same profound receptacles, are the Boatmen of our watering-place. Looking at them, you would say that surely these must be the laziest boatmen in the world. They lounge about, in obstinate and inflexible pantaloons that are apparently made of wood, the whole season through. Whether talking together about the shipping in the Channel, or gruffly unbending over mugs of beer at the public- house, you would consider them the slowest of men. The chances are a thousand to one that you might stay here for ten seasons, and never see a boatman in a hurry. A certain expression about his loose hands, when they are not in his pockets, as if he were carrying a considerable lump of iron in each, without any inconvenience, suggests strength, but he never seems to use it. He has the appearance of perpetually strolling - running is too inappropriate a word to be thought of - to seed. The only subject on which he seems to feel any approach to enthusiasm, is pitch. He pitches everything he can lay hold of, - the pier, the palings, his boat, his house, - when there is nothing else left he turns to and even pitches his hat, or his rough-weather clothing. Do not judge him by deceitful appearances. These are among the bravest and most skilful mariners that exist. Let a gale arise and swell into a storm, let a sea run that might appal the stoutest heart that ever beat, let the Light-boat on these dangerous sands throw up a rocket in the night, or let them hear through the angry roar the signal- guns of a ship in distress, and these men spring up into activity so dauntless, so valiant, and heroic, that the world cannot surpass it. Cavillers may object that they chiefly live upon the salvage of valuable cargoes. So they do, and God knows it is no great living that they get out of the deadly risks they run. But put that hope of gain aside. Let these rough fellows be asked, in any storm, who volunteers for the life-boat to save some perishing souls, as poor and empty-handed as themselves, whose lives the perfection of human reason does not rate at the value of a farthing each; and that boat will be manned, as surely and as cheerfully, as if a thousand pounds were told down on the weather-beaten pier. For this, and for the recollection of their comrades whom we have known, whom the raging sea has engulfed before their children's eyes in such brave efforts, whom the secret sand has buried, we hold the boatmen of our watering-place in our love and honour, and are tender of the fame they well deserve.

So many children are brought down to our watering-place that, when they are not out of doors, as they usually are in fine weather, it is wonderful where they are put: the whole village seeming much too small to hold them under cover. In the afternoons, you see no end of salt and sandy little boots drying on upper window-sills. At bathing-time in the morning, the little bay re-echoes with every shrill variety of shriek and splash - after which, if the weather be at all fresh, the sands teem with small blue mottled legs. The sands are the children's great resort. They cluster there, like ants: so busy burying their particular friends, and making castles with infinite labour which the next tide overthrows, that it is curious to consider how their play, to the music of the sea, foreshadows the realities of their after lives.

It is curious, too, to observe a natural ease of approach that there seems to be between the children and the boatmen. They mutually make acquaintance, and take individual likings, without any help. You will come upon one of those slow heavy fellows sitting down patiently mending a little ship for a mite of a boy, whom he could crush to death by throwing his lightest pair of trousers on him. You will be sensible of the oddest contrast between the smooth little creature, and the rough man who seems to be carved out of hard-grained wood - between the delicate hand expectantly held out, and the immense thumb and finger that can hardly feel the rigging of thread they mend - between the small voice and the gruff growl - and yet there is a natural propriety in the companionship: always to be noted in confidence between a child and a person who has any merit of reality and genuineness: which is admirably pleasant.

We have a preventive station at our watering-place, and much the same thing may be observed - in a lesser degree, because of their official character - of the coast blockade; a steady, trusty, well- conditioned, well-conducted set of men, with no misgiving about looking you full in the face, and with a quiet thorough-going way of passing along to their duty at night, carrying huge sou'-

wester clothing in reserve, that is fraught with all good prepossession. They are handy fellows - neat about their houses - industrous at gardening - would get on with their wives, one thinks, in a desert island - and people it, too, soon.

As to the naval officer of the station, with his hearty fresh face, and his blue eye that has pierced all kinds of weather, it warms our hearts when he comes into church on a Sunday, with that bright mixture of blue coat, buff waistcoat, black neck-kerchief, and gold epaulette, that is associated in the minds of all Englishmen with brave, unpretending, cordial, national service. We like to look at him in his Sunday state; and if we were First Lord (really possessing the indispensable qualification for the office of knowing nothing whatever about the sea), we would give him a ship to-morrow.

We have a church, by-the-by, of course - a hideous temple of flint, like a great petrified haystack. Our chief clerical dignitary, who, to his honour, has done much for education both in time and money, and has established excellent schools, is a sound, shrewd, healthy gentleman, who has got into little occasional difficulties with the neighbouring farmers, but has had a pestilent trick of being right. Under a new regulation, he has yielded the church of our watering-place to another clergyman. Upon the whole we get on in church well. We are a little bilious sometimes, about these days of fraternisation, and about nations arriving at a new and more unprejudiced knowledge of each other (which our Christianity don't quite approve), but it soon goes off, and then we get on very well.

There are two dissenting chapels, besides, in our small watering- place; being in about the proportion of a hundred and twenty guns to a yacht. But the dissension that has torn us lately, has not been a religious one. It has arisen on the novel question of Gas. Our watering-place has been convulsed by the agitation, Gas or No Gas. It was never reasoned why No Gas, but there was a great No Gas party. Broadsides were printed and stuck about - a startling circumstance in our watering-place. The No Gas party rested content with chalking 'No Gas!' and 'Down with Gas!' and other such angry war-whoops, on the few back gates and scraps of wall which the limits of our watering-place afford; but the Gas party printed and posted bills, wherein they took the high ground of proclaiming against the No Gas party, that it was said Let there be light and there was light; and that not to have light (that is gas-light) in our watering-place, was to contravene the great decree. Whether by these thunderbolts or not, the No Gas party were defeated; and in this present season we have had our handful of shops illuminated for the first time. Such of the No Gas party, however, as have got shops, remain in opposition and burn tallow - exhibiting in their windows the very picture of the sulkiness that punishes itself, and a new illustration of the old adage about cutting off your nose to be revenged on your face, in cutting off their gas to be revenged on their business.

Other population than we have indicated, our watering-place has none. There are a few old used-up boatmen who creep about in the sunlight with the help of sticks, and there is a poor imbecile shoemaker who wanders his lonely life away among the rocks, as if he were looking for his reason - which he will never find. Sojourners in neighbouring watering-places come occasionally in flys to stare at us, and drive away again as if they thought us very dull; Italian boys come, Punch comes, the Fantoccini come, the Tumblers come, the Ethiopians come; Glee-singers come at night, and hum and vibrate (not always melodiously) under our windows. But they all go soon, and leave us to ourselves again. We once had a travelling Circus and Wombwell's Menagerie at the same time. They both know better than ever to try it again; and the Menagerie had nearly razed us from the face of the earth in getting the elephant away - his caravan was so large, and the watering-place so small. We have a fine sea, wholesome for all people; profitable for the body, profitable for the mind. The poet's words are sometimes on its awful lips:

>   And the stately ships go on
>   To their haven under the hill;
>   But O for the touch of a vanish'd hand.
>   And the sound of a voice that is still!
>   Break, break, break,

> At the foot of thy crags, O sea!
> But the tender grace of a day that is dead
> Will never come back to me.

Yet it is not always so, for the speech of the sea is various, and wants not abundant resource of cheerfulness, hope, and lusty encouragement. And since I have been idling at the window here, the tide has risen. The boats are dancing on the bubbling water; the colliers are afloat again; the white-bordered waves rush in; the children

> Do chase the ebbing Neptune, and do fly him
> When he comes back;

> the radiant sails are gliding past the shore, and shining on the
> far horizon; all the sea is sparkling, heaving, swelling up with
> life and beauty, this bright morning.

Although Dickens no longer visited Broadstairs after 1851, his name lived on in the town, growing ever stronger as time went by, to such an extent that Broadstairs almost came to have as its sub-title 'Dickens-on-Sea'. Over time, the titles of his novels, his characters and even phrases that he made famous have so thoroughly colonized the town that they have formed a self-perpetuating species which continually evolves and reproduces in the names of streets, cafés, pubs, shops, hotels, private houses and assorted buildings, from flats to school. The survival of this species seems guaranteed, and it is safe to say that this part of the isle at least forever belongs to England's great novelist.

The 'queer old wooden pier', Broadstairs

View from Broadstairs pier today, with the skyline still much as Dickens would have seen it

CHAPTER SIX

PART OF THE PLOT

WILKIE COLLINS

It was Charles Dickens who first brought his young writer friend, **Wilkie Collins** (1824 - 1889), to Thanet and Collins, in need of sea air for his health, soon picked up the seaside habit. He came often, staying with Dickens on invitation initially, in Broadstairs, then coming on his own account for his stays on the coast. It was in the still existing Church Hill Cottage at the Broadstairs end of Ramsgate Road that he began writing his most famous suspense novel and great masterpiece, *The Woman in White,* in company with the real-life model for the heroine, Caroline Graves, and it was the dazzlingly white North Foreland lighthouse nearby that reputedly triggered in his mind the title of his story.

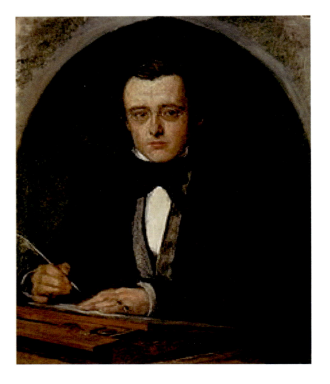

Portrait of Wilkie Collins, aged 29, by his brother Charles Allston Collins

Collins eventually gravitated on to Ramsgate from Broadstairs. Broadstairs had lost something of its appeal, especially as Dickens no longer came for his extended stays, and Collins' enthusiasm for sailing made the prospect of Ramsgate's large harbour with its yacht club, which he joined, a much more attractive proposition. This unconventional Victorian with a claustrophobic fear of marrying was also enthusiastic about bringing his two mistresses to Ramsgate, famously installing one household in Nelson Crescent, and the other totally separately on the other side of the bay in Wellington Crescent.

Although none of the action of his most well-known early novels takes place in Thanet, large chunks of the narrative of his later novels are set in the Ramsgate he got to know so well. Collins' trademark was what was called 'sensation', which, translated into today's terms, would be 'suspense'. His page-turning plots became ever more convoluted in his later novels, with ever stronger doses of social documenting, and Ramsgate becomes a vividly evoked background scene in the unfolding twists of these stories.

In *Poor Miss Finch* (1872) the wealthy young Lucilla Finch, blind from childhood, falls in love with Oscar, a man who has developed epilepsy after being attacked during a robbery. The cure for Oscar involves large amounts silver nitrate which turns his face blue, and when Oscar's twin brother, Nugent, returns penniless from abroad he manoeuvres Lucilla, who has temporarily regained her sight following treatment, into believing he is Oscar so that he can marry her and get his hands on her money. As Oscar owes Nugent his life due to an earlier incident, and especially as he does not want Lucilla to feel revulsed by his blue face, he leaves England and lets Nugent impersonate him. Nugent, maintaining the deception, recommends taking the air in Ramsgate as part of Lucilla's treatment, trying at the same time to keep out of the public eye. But Lucilla feels there is something wrong, and, while in Ramsgate, notes as much in her journal, where she, of course, mistakenly refers to Nugent as Oscar.

From *Poor Miss Finch* (1872):

I proposed returning by the sands. Ramsgate is still crowded with visitors; and the animated scene on the beach in the later part of the day has attractions for me, after my blind life, which it does not (I dare say) possess for people who have always enjoyed the use of their eyes. Oscar, who has a nervous horror of crowds, and who shrinks from contact with people not so refined as himself, was surprised at my wishing to mix with what he called "the mob on the sands." However, he said he would go, if I particularly wished it. I did particularly wish it. So we went.

There were chairs on the beach. We hired two, and sat down to look about us.

All sorts of diversions were going on. Monkeys, organs, girls on stilts, a conjurer, and a troop of negro minstrels, were all at work to amuse the visitors. I thought the varied colour and bustling enjoyment of the crowd, with the bright blue sea beyond, and the glorious sunshine overhead, quite delightful—I declare I felt as if two eyes were not half enough to see with! A nice old lady, sitting near, entered into conversation with me; hospitably offering me biscuits and sherry out of her own bag. Oscar, to my disappointment, looked quite disgusted with all of us. He thought my nice old lady vulgar; and he called the company on the beach "a herd of snobs." While he was still muttering under his breath about the "mixture of low people," he suddenly cast a side-look at some person or thing—I could not at the moment tell which—and, rising, placed himself so as to intercept my view of the promenade on the sands immediately before me. I happened to have noticed, at the same moment, a lady approaching us in a dress of a peculiar colour; and I pulled Oscar on one side, to look at her as she passed in front of me. "Why do you get in my way?" I asked. Before he could answer the question the lady passed, with two lovely children, and with a tall man at her side. My eyes, looking first at the lady and the children, found their way next to the gentleman—and saw repeated in his face, the same black-blue complexion which had startled me in the face of Oscar's brother, when I first opened my eyes at the rectory! For the moment I felt startled again—more, as I believe, by the unexpected repetition of the blue face in the face of a stranger, than by the ugliness of the complexion itself. At any rate, I was composed enough to admire the lady's dress, and the beauty of the children, before they had passed beyond my range of view. Oscar spoke to me, while I was looking at them, in a tone of reproach for which, as I thought, there was no occasion and no excuse.

"I tried to spare you," he said. "You have yourself to thank, if that man has frightened you."

"He has *not* frightened me," I answered—sharply enough.

Oscar looked at me very attentively; and sat down again, without saying a word more.

The good-humoured old woman, on my other side, who had seen and heard all that had passed, began to talk of the gentleman with the discoloured face, and of the lady and the children who accompanied him. He was a retired Indian officer, she said. The lady was his wife, and the two beautiful children were his own children. "It seems a pity that such a handsome man should be disfigured in that way," my new acquaintance remarked. "But still, it don't matter much, after all. There he is, as you see, with a fine woman for a wife, and with two lovely children. I know the landlady of the house where they lodge—and a happier family you couldn't lay your hand on in all England. That is my friend's account of them. Even a blue face don't seem such a dreadful misfortune, when you look at it in that light—does it, Miss?"

Ramsgate figures much more largely in Collins' novel, *The Law and the Lady* (1875). Once again in true Collins style we have a strong and determined female protagonist in the shape of Valeria Woodville, giving the novel a very modern feel, especially as she proves a far stronger character than her husband, Eustace, who she has just married at the start of the story. Valeria and Eustace take the train to Ramsgate for their honeymoon so that they can board the yacht lent to them by a friend for a cruise of the Mediterranean – a reflection here of Collins' membership of Ramsgate's Royal Temple Yacht Club and his own yachting jaunts with his friend Edward Pigott.

At Ramsgate Valeria has an unpleasant encounter on the sands with her new mother-in-law, who informs her of a dark secret in her husband's past. Further aspects of this past come to light in Ramsgate and the story then moves into Valeria's long quest to prove her husband's innocence in a case where, she learns, he was accused of murdering his first wife but where the case was concluded as unproven. The 'unproven' verdict leaves a shadow hanging over Eustace and, while he flees abroad to get away from his past, Valeria turns herself into an amateur detective to get to the truth in the hope of saving their marriage. Here we find the initially happy couple just arriving in Ramsgate.

From *The Law and the Lady* (1875)*:*

We left the train at Ramsgate.

The favourite watering-place was empty; the season was just over. Our arrangements for the wedding tour included a cruise to the Mediterranean in a yacht lent to Eustace by a friend. We were both fond of the sea, and we were equally desirous, considering the circumstances under which we had married, of escaping the notice of friends and acquaintances. With this object in view, having celebrated our marriage privately in London, we had decided on instructing the sailing-master of the yacht to join us at Ramsgate. At this port (when the season for visitors was at an end) we could embark far more privately than at the popular yachting stations situated in the Isle of Wight.

Three days passed—days of delicious solitude, of exquisite happiness, never to be forgotten, never to be lived over again, to the end of our lives!

Early on the morning of the fourth day, just before sunrise, a trifling incident happened, which was noticeable, nevertheless, as being strange to me in my experience of myself.

I awoke, suddenly and unaccountably, from a deep and dreamless sleep with an all-pervading sensation of nervous uneasiness which I had never felt before. In the old days at the Vicarage my capacity as a sound sleeper had been the subject of many a little harmless joke. From the moment when my head was on the pillow I had never known what it was to awake until the maid knocked at my door. At all seasons and times the long and uninterrupted repose of a child was the repose that I enjoyed.

And now I had awakened, without any assignable cause, hours before my usual time. I tried to compose myself to sleep again. The effort was useless. Such a restlessness possessed me that I was not even able to lie still in the bed. My husband was sleeping soundly by my side. In the fear of disturbing him I rose, and put on my dressing-gown and slippers.

I went to the window. The sun was just rising over the calm grey sea. For a while the majestic spectacle before me exercised a tranquillizing influence on the irritable condition of my nerves. But ere long the old restlessness returned upon me. I walked slowly to and fro in the room, until I was weary of the monotony of the exercise. I took up a book, and laid it aside again. My attention wandered; the author was powerless to recall it. I got on my feet once more, and looked at Eustace, and admired him and loved him in his tranquil sleep. I went back to the window, and wearied of the beautiful morning. I sat down before the glass and looked at myself. How haggard and worn I was already, through awaking before my usual time! I rose again, not knowing what to do next. The confinement to the four walls of the room began to be intolerable to me. I opened the door that led into my husband's dressing-room, and entered it, to try if the change would relieve me.

The first object that I noticed was his dressing-case, open on the toilet-table.

I took out the bottles and pots and brushes and combs, the knives and scissors in one compartment, the writing materials in another. I smelled the perfumes and pomatums; I busily cleaned and dusted the bottles with my handkerchief as I took them out. Little by little I completely emptied the dressing-case. It was lined with blue velvet. In one corner I noticed a tiny slip of loose blue silk. Taking it between my finger and thumb, and drawing it upward, I discovered that there was a false bottom to the case, forming a secret compartment for letters and papers. In my strange condition—capricious, idle, inquisitive—it was an amusement to me to take out the papers, just as I had taken out everything else.

I found some receipted bills, which failed to interest me; some letters, which it is needless to say I laid aside after only looking at the addresses; and, under all, a photograph, face downward, with writing on the back of it. I looked at the writing, and saw these words:

"To my dear son, Eustace."

His mother! the woman who had so obstinately and mercilessly opposed herself to our marriage!

I eagerly turned the photograph, expecting to see a woman with a stern, ill-tempered, forbidding countenance. To my surprise, the face showed the remains of great beauty; the expression, though remarkably firm, was yet winning, tender, and kind. The grey hair was arranged in rows of little quaint old-fashioned curls on either side of the head, under a plain lace cap. At one corner of the mouth there was a mark, apparently a mole, which added to the characteristic peculiarity of the face. I looked and looked, fixing the portrait thoroughly in my mind. This woman, who had almost insulted me and my relatives, was, beyond all doubt or dispute, so far as appearances went, a person possessing unusual attractions—a person whom it would be a pleasure and a privilege to know.

I fell into deep thought. The discovery of the photograph quieted me as nothing had quieted me yet.

The striking of a clock downstairs in the hall warned me of the flight of time. I carefully put back all the objects in the dressing-case (beginning with the photograph) exactly as I had found them, and returned to the bedroom. As I looked at my husband, still sleeping peacefully, the question forced itself into my mind: what had made that genial, gentle mother of his so sternly bent on parting us? So harshly and pitilessly resolute in asserting her disapproval of our marriage?

Could I put my question openly to Eustace when he awoke? No; I was afraid to venture that length. It had been tacitly understood between us that we were not to speak of his mother—and, besides, he might be angry if he knew that I had opened the private compartment of his dressing-case.

After breakfast that morning we had news at last of the yacht. The vessel was safely moored in the inner harbour, and the sailing-master was waiting to receive my husband's orders on board.

Eustace hesitated at asking me to accompany him to the yacht. It would be necessary for him to examine the inventory of the vessel, and to decide questions, not very interesting to a woman, relating to charts and barometers, provisions and water. He asked me if I would wait for his return. The day was enticingly beautiful, and the tide was on the ebb. I pleaded for a walk on the sands; and the landlady at our lodgings, who happened to be in the room at the time, volunteered to accompany me and take care of me. It was agreed that we should walk as far as we felt inclined in the direction of Broadstairs, and that Eustace should follow and meet us on the sands, after having completed his arrangements on board the yacht.

In half an hour more the landlady and I were out on the beach.

The scene on that fine autumn morning was nothing less than enchanting. The brisk breeze, the brilliant sky, the flashing blue sea, the sun-bright cliffs and the tawny sands at their feet, the gliding procession of ships on the great marine highway of the English Channel—it was all so exhilarating, it was all so delightful, that I really believe if I had been by myself I could have danced for joy like a child. The one drawback to my happiness was the landlady's untiring tongue. She was a forward, good-natured, empty-headed woman, who persisted in talking, whether I listened or not, and who had a habit of perpetually addressing me as "Mrs. Woodville," which I thought a little overfamiliar as an assertion of equality from a person in her position to a person in mine.

We had been out, I should think, more than half an hour, when we overtook a lady walking before us on the beach.

Just as we were about to pass the stranger she took her handkerchief from her pocket, and accidentally drew out with it a letter, which fell unnoticed by her, on the sand. I was nearest to the letter, and I picked it up and offered it to the lady.

The instant she turned to thank me, I stood rooted to the spot. There was the original of the photographic portrait in the dressing-case! There was my husband's mother, standing face to face with me! I recognized the quaint little grey curls, the gentle, genial expression, the mole at the corner of the mouth. No mistake was possible. His mother herself!

The Port of Ramsgate

Ramsgate reappears as that useful nether-world repository of secrecy and secret activities in Collins' 1879 novel, *The Fallen Leaves*. The extraordinary, not to say incredibility-stretching, plot of the novel is set in motion in the town in the introductory Prologue, which narrates events that took place sixteen years before the story proper.

The 'fallen leaves' in question are fallen women, those sad creatures of Victorian art and fiction who are both despised and pitied in equal measure. In the story, the American protagonist, Amelius Goldenheart, is accosted by a sixteen-year-old prostitute in London, gives her shelter, falls in love with her and at the end of the story marries her, in spite of having previously been engaged to the niece of the villain of the piece, John Farnaby. It turns out that Sally, the prostitute, is, by one of those typical Wilkie Collins coincidences, the illegitimate child of John Farnaby's wife, who was seduced by Farnaby prior to their marriage and who had the baby in secret in Ramsgate sixteen years earlier.

In the Prologue's backstory we discover the circumstances of the birth. Shop assistant Farnaby, having calculated that by making his boss's daughter pregnant he would further his career prospects at the shop, comes to Ramsgate to find and abduct the baby and hand her over to a baby farmer. He follows his boss, Benjamin Ronald, who has taken the train to Ramsgate to look for his wife and daughter. His wife has said she has taken her daughter to Ramsgate for health reasons and has not told him she was pregnant and that she has now given birth. We pick up the story as Benjamin Ronald searches for his wife in Ramsgate, who is not at the address she had given him. He has been directed to another address, and is secretly followed by Farnaby.

From *The Fallen Leaves* (1879):

The blue lustre of the sky was without a cloud; the sunny sea leapt under the fresh westerly breeze. From the beach, the cries of children at play, the shouts of donkey-boys driving their poor beasts, the distant notes of brass instruments playing a waltz, and the mellow music of the small waves breaking on the sand, rose joyously together on the fragrant air. On the next bench, a dirty old boatman was prosing to a stupid old visitor. Mr. Ronald listened, with a sense of vacant content in the mere act of listening. The boatman's words found their way to his ears like the other sounds that were abroad in the air. Yes; them's the Goodwin Sands, where you see the lightship. And that steamer there, towing a vessel into the harbour, that's the Ramsgate Tug. Do you know what I should like to see? I should like to see the Ramsgate Tug blow up. Why? I'll tell you why. I belong to Broadstairs; I don't belong to Ramsgate. Very well. I'm idling here, as you may see, without one copper piece in my pocket to rub against another. What trade do I belong to? I don't belong to no trade; I belong to a boat. The boat's rotting at Broadstairs, for want of work. And all along of what? All along of the Tug. The Tug has took the bread out of our mouths: me and my mates. Wait a bit; I'll show you how. What did a ship do, in the good old times, when she got on them Goodwin Sands? Went to pieces, if it come on to blow; or got sucked down little by little when it was fair weather. Now I'm coming to it. What did We do (in the good old times, mind you) when we happened to see that ship in distress? Out with our boat; blow high or blow low, out with our boat. And saved the lives of the crew, did you say? Well, yes; saving the crew was part of the day's work, to be sure; the part we didn't get paid for. We saved the cargo, Master! and got salvage!! Hundreds of pounds, I tell you, divided amongst us by law!!! Ah, those times are gone. A parcel of sneaks get together, and subscribe to build a Steam-Tug. When a ship gets on the sands now, out goes the Tug, night and day alike, and brings her safe into harbour, and takes the bread out of our mouths. Shameful that's what I call it, shameful.

The Ramsgate Tug

The last words of the boatman's lament fell lower, lower, lower on Mr. Ronald's ears. He lost them altogether, he lost the view of the sea, he lost the sense of the wind blowing over him. Suddenly, he was roused as if from a deep sleep. On one side, the man from Broadstairs was shaking him by the collar. I say, Master, cheer up; what's come to you? On the other side, a compassionate lady was offering her smelling-bottle. I am afraid, sir, you have fainted. He struggled to his feet, and vacantly thanked the lady. The man from Broadstairs with an eye to salvage took charge of the human wreck, and towed him to the nearest public-house. A chop and a glass of brandy-and-water, said this good Samaritan of the nineteenth century. That's what you want. I'm peckish myself, and I'll keep you company. He was perfectly passive in the hands of any one who would take charge of him; he submitted as if he had been the boatman's dog, and had heard the whistle. It could only be truly said that he had come to himself, when there had been time enough for him to feel the reanimating influence of the food and drink. Then he got to his feet, and looked with incredulous wonder at the companion of his meal. The man from Broadstairs opened his greasy lips, and was silenced by the sudden appearance of a gold coin between Mr. Ronald's finger and thumb. Don't speak to me; pay the bill, and bring me the change outside. When the boatman joined him, he was reading a letter; walking to and fro, and speaking at intervals to himself. God help me, have I lost my senses? I don't know what to do next. He referred to the letter again: if you don't believe me, ask Mrs. Turner, Number 1, Slains Row, Ramsgate. He put the letter back in his pocket, and rallied suddenly. Slains Row, he said, turning to the boatman. Take me there directly, and keep the change for yourself. The boatman's gratitude was (apparently) beyond expression in words. He slapped his pocket cheerfully, and that was all. Leading the way inland, he went downhill, and uphill again, then turned aside towards the eastern extremity of the town. Farnaby, still following, with the woman behind him, stopped when the boatman diverged towards the east, and looked up at the name of the street. I've got my instructions, he said; I know where he's going. Step out! We'll get there before him, by another way. Mr. Ronald and his guide reached a row of poor little houses, with poor little gardens in front of them and behind them. The back windows looked out on downs and fields lying on either side of the road to Broadstairs. It was a lost and lonely spot. The guide stopped, and put a question with inquisitive respect. What number, sir? Mr. Ronald had sufficiently recovered himself to keep his own counsel. That will do, he said. You can leave me. The boatman waited a moment. Mr. Ronald looked at him. The boatman was slow to understand that his leadership had gone from him. You're sure you don't want me any more? he said. Quite sure, Mr. Ronald answered. The man from Broadstairs retired with his salvage to comfort him. Number 1 was at the farther extremity of the row of houses. When Mr. Ronald rang the bell, the spies were already posted. The woman loitered on the road, within view of the door. Farnaby was out of sight, round the corner, watching the house over the low wooden palings of the back garden. A lazy-looking man, in his shirt sleeves, opened the door. Mrs. Turner at home? he repeated. Well, she's at home; but she's too busy to see anybody. What's your pleasure? Mr. Ronald declined to accept excuses or to answer questions. I must see Mrs. Turner directly, he said, on important business. His tone and manner had their effect on the lazy man. What name? he asked. Mr.

Ronald declined to mention his name. Give my message, he said. I won't detain Mrs. Turner more than a minute. The man hesitated and opened the door of the front parlour. An old woman was fast asleep on a ragged little sofa. The man gave up the front parlour, and tried the back parlour next. It was empty. Please to wait here, he said and went away to deliver his message.

The parlour was a miserably furnished room. Through the open window, the patch of back garden was barely visible under fluttering rows of linen hanging out on lines to dry. A pack of dirty cards, and some plain needlework, littered the bare little table. A cheap American clock ticked with stern and steady activity on the mantelpiece. The smell of onions was in the air. A torn newspaper, with stains of beer on it, lay on the floor. There was some sinister influence in the place which affected Mr. Ronald painfully. He felt himself trembling, and sat down on one of the rickety chairs. The minutes followed one another wearily. He heard a trampling of feet in the room above, then a door opened and closed, then the rustle of a woman's dress on the stairs. In a moment more, the handle of the parlour door was turned. He rose, in anticipation of Mrs. Turner's appearance. The door opened. He found himself face to face with his wife**.**

Collins shows his usual mastery in depicting the Ramsgate scenes, with an old sea salt nicely portrayed along with his complaint about the newfangled steam-tug that has taken away his livelihood. The only obviously fictional element in his realistic evocation is the street, Slains Row, which is invented. Unfortunately, the realism of Collins' descriptions was not matched by the realism of his plot and the book was not a great success. It is worth noting, however, that Collins almost pioneered the concept of plot in suspense novels and, generally, there was a great willingness on the part of the Victorian public to suspend disbelief in the highly fanciful turn of events and bizarre coincidences of his stories. The plot was accepted as a new and fascinating structure, and it is only much later that the public looked for more realistic plots. Nonetheless, even the Victorian reader started to balk at the plot of *The Fallen Leaves*, with the additional problem that the book had an active prostitute (rather than the more acceptable ex-prostitute) as a heroine - a step too far for the times.

CHAPTER SEVEN

SEA DRAMA

R M BALLANTYNE

The Scottish writer **Robert Michael Ballantyne** (1825 - 1894), an exact contemporary of Wilkie Collins, also came to Ramsgate in the early 1860s and incorporated the Thanet seascapes, especially the feared Goodwin Sands, into his writing. Ballantyne was a very different writer from Collins and, writing adventure stories for the young audience of the mid nineteenth century, he was particularly interested in the dramas of the stormy seas of the English Channel. Ramsgate provided the ideal base for his research.

R M Ballantyne

The fruit of these investigations came in the shape of two books, *The Lifeboat* (1864) and *The Floating Light of the Goodwin Sands* (1870). In the Preface to the latter book, Ballantyne names and fully acknowledges the various men in Ramsgate connected with the lifeboats and the lightships of that part of the coast who directly informed him of their work, and indeed he expresses his gratitude for being given the opportunity to join the crew of the *Gull* lightship to gain first hand experience.

This 'hands-on' approach to writing characterized Ballantyne, who travelled widely, including five years in Canada working for the Hudson Bay Company. He used all his experience in so many places, ground up in his powerful imagination, to produce over one hundred adventure books aimed at young people during his lifetime, all very much within the brave, heroic British Empire-building spirit of the times. His most famous and enduring novel, *The Coral Island,* concerns three boys marooned on a South Pacific island after a shipwreck who show great qualities of organizational resourcefulness and self-reliance as they battle for survival.   The story directly inspired Robert Louis Stevenson's *Treasure Island* as well as many of the stories in Edwin J Brett's popular weekly adventure periodicals *Boys of England*.

   A great deal of physical strength, skill and resourcefulness was certainly a necessary attribute of the crew of the *Gull* lightship, a day in whose life is vividly evoked in *The Floating Light of the Goodwin Sands*. As the title suggests, the Goodwin Sands figure prominently again in this novel, and we are reminded of the Ramsgate boatman in Wilkie Collins' *The Fallen Leaves* who elaborates at length on these terrifying sands and mentions the lightship, as well as vehemently railing against the very same steam-tug that appears in this earlier story of Ballantyne's (see Chapter Six).

   We join the crew of the *Gull* as they are alerted to a ship in distress on the sands and take action to send the signal for the lifeboat.

From *The Floating Light of the Goodwin Sands* (1870):

Jack Shales dived down the companion-hatch, and in another moment returned with a red-hot poker, which the mate had thrust into the cabin fire at the first alarm. He applied it in quick succession to the gun and rocket. A blinding flash and deafening crash were followed by the whiz of the rocket as it sprang with a magnificent curve far away into the surrounding darkness.

This was their answer to the South sandhead light, which, having fired three guns and sent up three rockets to attract the attention of the Gull, then ceased firing. It was also their first note of warning to the look-out on the pier of Ramsgate harbour. Of the three light-ships that guarded the sands, the Gull lay nearest to Ramsgate; hence, whichever of the other two happened to send up signals, the Gull had to reply and thenceforward to continue repeating them until the attention of the Ramsgate look-out should be gained, and a reply given.

"That's a beauty," cried the mate, referring to the rocket; "fetch another, Jack; sponge her well out, Dick Moy, we'll give 'em another shot in a few minutes."

Loud and clear were both the signals, but four and a half miles of distance and a fresh gale neutralised their influence. The look-out on the pier did not observe them. In less than five minutes the gun and rocket were fired again. Still no answering signal came from Ramsgate.

"Load the weather gun this time," cried the mate, "they'll have a better chance of seeing the flash of that."

Jack obeyed, and Jim Welton, having nothing to do but look on, sought shelter under the lee of the weather bulwarks, for the wind, according to Dick Moy, "was blowin' needles and penknives."

The third gun thundered forth and shook the floating light from stem to stern, but the rocket struck the rigging and made a low wavering flight. Another was therefore sent up, but it had scarcely cut its bright line across the sky when the answering signal was observed—a rocket from Ramsgate pier!

"That's all right now; *our* duty's done," said the mate, as he went below, and, divesting himself of his outer garments, quietly turned in, while the watch, having sponged out and re-covered the guns, resumed their active perambulation of the deck.

James Welton, however, could not calm down his feelings so easily. This was the first night he had ever spent in a light-ship; the scene was therefore quite new to him, and he could not help feeling somewhat disappointed at the sudden termination of the noise and excitement. He was told that the Ramsgate lifeboat could not be out in less than an hour, and it seemed to his excited spirit a terrible thing that human lives should be kept so long in jeopardy. Of course he began to think, "Is it not possible to prevent this delay?" but his better sense whispered to him that excited spirits are not the best judges in such matters, although it cannot be denied that they have an irresistible tendency to judge. There was nothing for it, however, but to exercise philosophic patience, so he went below and turned in, as sailors have it, "all standing," to be ready when the lifeboat should make its appearance.

The young sailor's sleep was prompt and profound. It seemed to him but a few minutes after he had laid his head on the pillow when Jack Shale's voice again resounded in the cabin—

"Lifeboat close alongside, sir. Didn't see her till this moment. She carries no lights."

The Weltons, father and son, sprang out of their bunks a second time, and, minus coat, hat, and shoes, scrambled on deck just in time to see the Broadstairs lifeboat rush past before the gale. She was close under the stern, and rendered spectrally visible by the light of the lantern.

"What are you firing for?" shouted the coxswain of the boat.

"Ship on the sands, bearing south," roared Jack Shales at the full pitch of his stentorian voice.

There was no time for more, for the boat did not pause in her meteor-like flight. The question was asked and answered as she passed with a magnificent rush into darkness. The reply had been heard, and the lifeboat shot, straight as an arrow, to the rescue.

Reader, we often hear and read of such scenes, but we can tell you from experience that vision is necessary to enable one to realise the full import of all that goes on. There was a strange thrill at the heart of young Welton when he saw the familiar blue-and-white boat leaping over the foaming billows. Often had he seen it in model and in quiescence in its boat-house, ponderous and almost ungainly; but now he saw it for the first time in action, as if endued with life. So, we fancy, warriors might speak of our heavy cavalry as *we* see them in barracks and as *they* saw them at Alma.

Again all was silent and unexciting on board the Gull; but, not many minutes later, the watch once more shouted down the skylight—

"Tug's in sight, sir."

It was afterwards ascertained that a mistake had been made in reference to the vessel that had signalled. Some one on shore had reported that the guns and rockets had been seen flashing from the *North* sandhead vessel, whereas the report should have been, "from the vessel at the *South* sandhead." The single word was all-important. It had the effect of sending the steam-tug Aid (which always attends upon the Ramsgate lifeboat) in the wrong direction, involving much loss of time. But we mention this merely as a fact, not as a reproof. Accidents will happen, even in the best regulated families. The Ramsgate lifeboat service is most admirably regulated; and for once that an error of this kind can be pointed out, we can point to dozens—ay, hundreds—of cases in which the steamer and lifeboat have gone, straight as the crow flies, to the rescue, and have done good service on occasions when all other lifeboats would certainly have failed; so great is the value of steam in such matters.

On this occasion, however, the tug appeared somewhat late on the scene, and hailed the Gull. When the true state of the case was ascertained, her course was directed aright, and full steam let on. The Ramsgate boat was in tow far astern. As she passed, the brief questions and answers were repeated for the benefit of the coxswain, and Jim Welton observed that every man in the boat appeared to be crouching down on the thwarts except the coxswain, who stood at the steering tackles. No wonder. It is not an easy matter to sit up in a gale of wind, with freezing spray, and sometimes green seas, sweeping over one! The men were doubtless wideawake and listening, but, as far as vision went, that boat was manned by ten oilskin coats and sou'westers!

A few seconds carried them out of sight, and so great was the power of steam that, despite the loss of time, they reached the neighbourhood of the wreck as soon as the Broadstairs boat, and found that the crew of the stranded vessel had already been saved, and taken ashore by the Deal lifeboat.

Today the East Goodwin Lightship is one of five surviving lightships. The *Gull,* so dramatically described by Ballantyne in his novel, sadly sank in 1929 after being rammed accidentally, resulting in the death of its then captain. Fortunately, though, memory of the ship and its days off the coast of Thanet still persist, thanks entirely to the writing powers of R M Ballantyne.

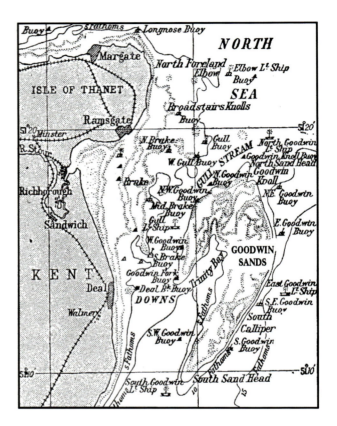

A chart showing the Goodwin Sands

The East Goodwin Lightship

CHAPTER EIGHT

SETTING FOR LOVE AND LIES

BARONESS ORCZY

Baroness Emmuska Orczy

Baroness Orczy (1865 – 1947), the Hungarian-born creator of the *Scarlet Pimpernel*, was an aspiring artist who came to realize her calling lay in writing rather than art. She was certainly right to change direction. And the phenomenal success of her Scarlet Pimpernel stories, to the consternation of the many publishers who initially rejected her, allowed her to move from London to Thanet for a happy three-year interlude of country air and quiet.

In addition to her Pimpernel stories, in which the so-called Pimpernel rescues aristocrats from *Madame Guillotine* in revolutionary France - and whose identity is in reality the superior Englishman, Sir Percy Blakeney - Orczy wrote a number of historical romances. Most of these are set abroad, simply because Orczy, although possessed of formidable skills in English, was afraid of getting an English name or point of geography wrong as she had not been brought up in England, only having come to this country as a teenager (and not speaking a word of English). However, one such historical romance is set in England, in Acol in Thanet, entitled *The Nest of the Sparrowhawk*.

Orczy was on surer ground with *The Nest of the Sparrowhawk*. She and her artist husband, Montague Barstow, had leased Cleve Court, a fine Georgian house on the Minster Road between Acol and Minster, and so she was well able to make use of her new Thanet surroundings as a setting for this romance. She takes us to the Cromwellian period after the English Civil War to find there a beautiful young heiress of noble family, orphaned in the war, and living under the guardianship of the impoverished, scheming owner of Acol Court, the name Orczy now gives to Cleve Court. She adds a trademark European dimension to the story by introducing a fake French prince, apparently living in exile in Acol. However, this prince is none other than the girl's guardian in disguise, who tries to get her to fall in love with his French prince-persona so that he can marry her and get his hands on her fortune.

Here, one evening in the grounds of the house, we meet the young heiress, Lady Sue, the penniless secretary, Richard Lambert, who is in love with her, and her repellent guardian, Sir Marmaduke de Chavasse masquerading in the shadows as the romantic Prince Amédé d'Orléans, with whom she girlishly fancies she is in love.

From *The Nest of the Sparrowhawk* (1909):

The dark figure of her guardian's secretary had attracted her attention from the moment when she first saw him moving silently about the house and park: the first words she spoke to him were words of sympathy. His life-story—brief and simple as it had been—had interested her. He seemed so different from these young and old country squires who frequented Acol Court. He neither wooed nor flattered her, yet seemed to find great joy in her company. His voice at times was harsh, his manner abrupt and even rebellious, but at others it fell to infinite gentleness when he talked to her of Nature and the stars, both of which he had studied deeply.

He never spoke of religion. That subject which was on everybody's tongue, together with the free use of the most sacred names, he rigorously avoided, also politics, and my Lord Protector's government, his dictatorship and ever-growing tyranny: but he knew the name of every flower that grew in meadow or woodland, the note of every bird as it trilled its song.

There is no doubt that but for the advent of that mysterious personality into Acol village, the deep friendship which had grown in Sue's heart for Richard Lambert would have warmed into a more passionate attachment.

But she was too young to reflect, too impulsive to analyse her feelings. The mystery which surrounded the foreigner who lodged at the Quakeress's cottage had made strong appeal to her idealism.

His first introduction to her notice, in the woods beyond the park gate on that cold January evening, with the moon gleaming weirdly through the branches of the elms, his solitary figure leaning against a tree, had fired her imagination and set it wildly galloping after mad fantasies.

He had scarcely spoken on that first occasion, but his silence was strangely impressive. She made up her mind that he was singularly handsome, although she could not judge of that very clearly for he wore a heavy moustache, and a shade over one eye; but he was tall, above the average, and carried the elaborate habiliments which the Cavaliers still affected, with consummate grace and ease. She thought, too, that the thick perruque became him very well, and his muffled voice, when he spoke, sounded singularly sweet.

Since then she had seen him constantly. At rare intervals at first, for maidenly dignity forbade that she should seem eager to meet him. He was ignorant of whom she was—oh! of that she felt quite quite sure: she always wore a dark tippet round her shoulders, and a hood to cover her head. He seemed pleased to see her, just to hear her voice. Obviously he was lonely and in deep trouble.

Then one night—it was the first balmy evening after the winter frosts—the moon was singularly bright, and the hood had fallen back from her head, just as her face was tilted upwards and her eyes glowing with enthusiasm. Then she knew that he had learnt to love her, not through any words which he spoke, for he was silent; his face was in shadow, and he did not even touch her; therefore it was not through any of her natural senses that she guessed his love. Yet she knew it, and her young heart was overfilled with happiness.

That evening when they parted he knelt at her feet and kissed the hem of her kirtle. After which, when she was back again in her own little room at Acol Court, she cried for very joy.

They did not meet very often. Once a week at most. He had vaguely promised to tell her, some day, of his great work for the regeneration of France, which he was carrying out in loneliness and exile here in England, a work far greater and more comprehensive than that which had secured for England religious and political liberty; this work it was which made him a wanderer on the face of the earth and caused his frequent and lengthy absences from the cottage in which he lodged.

She was quite content for the moment with these vague promises: in her heart she was evolving enchanting plans for the future, when she would be his helpmate in this great and mysterious work.

In the meanwhile she was satisfied to live in the present, to console and comfort the noble exile, to lavish on him the treasures of her young and innocent love, to endow him in her imagination with all those mental and physical attributes which her romantic nature admired most.

The spring had come, clothing the weird branches of the elms with a tender garb of green, the anemones in the woods yielded to the bluebells and these to carpets of primroses and violets. The forests of Thanet echoed with songs of linnets and white-throats. She was happy and she was in love.

With the lengthened days came some petty sorrows. He was obviously worried, sometimes even impatient. Their meetings became fewer and shorter, for the evening hours were brief. She found it difficult to wander out so late across the park, unperceived, and he would never meet her by day-light.

This no doubt had caused him to fret. He loved her and desired her all his own. Yet 'twere useless of a surety to ask Sir Marmaduke's consent to her marriage with her French prince. He would never give it, and until she came of age he had absolute power over her choice of a husband.

She had explained this to him and he had sighed and murmured angry words, then pressed her with increased passion to his heart.

To-night as she walked through the park, she was conscious—for the first time perhaps—of a certain alloy mixed with her gladness. Yet she loved him—oh, yes! just, just as much as ever. The halo of romance with which she had framed in his mystic personality was in no way dimmed, but in a sense she almost feared him, for at times his muffled voice sounded singularly vehement, and his words betrayed the uncontrolled violence of his nature.

She had hoped to bring him some reassuring news anent Sir Marmaduke de Chavasse's intentions with regard to herself, but the conversation round the skittle-alley, her guardian's cruel allusions to "the foreign adventurer," had shown her how futile were such hopes.

Yet, there were only three months longer of this weary waiting. Surely he could curb his impatience until she was of age and mistress of her own hand! Surely he trusted her!

She sighed as this thought crossed her mind, and nearly fell up against a dark figure which detached itself from among the trees.

"Master Lambert!" she said, uttering a little cry of surprise, pressing her hand against her heart which was palpitating with emotion. "I had no thought of meeting you here."

"And I still less of seeing your ladyship," he rejoined coldly.

"How cross you are," she retorted with childish petulance, "what have I done that you should be so unkind?"

"Unkind?"

"Aye! I had meant to speak to you of this ere now—but you always avoid me ... you scarce will look at me ... and ... and I wished to ask you if I had offended you?"

They were standing on a soft carpet of moss, overhead the gentle summer breeze stirred the great branches of the elms, causing the crisp leaves to mutter a long-drawn hush-sh-sh in the stillness of the night. From far away came the appealing call of a blackbird chased by some marauding owl, while on the ground close by, the creaking of tiny branches betrayed the quick scurrying of a squirrel. From the remote and infinite distance came the subdued roar of the sea.

The peace of the woodland, the sighing of the trees, the dark evening sky above, filled his heart with an aching longing for her.

"Offended me?" he murmured, passing his hand across his forehead, for his temples throbbed and his eyes were burning. "Nay! why should you think so?"

"You are so cold, so distant now," she said gently. "We were such good friends when first I came here. Thanet is a strange country to me. It seems weird and unkind—the woods are dark and lonely, that persistent sound of the sea fills me with a strange kind of dread. ... My home was among the Surrey hills you know. ... It is far from here. ... I cannot afford to lose a friend. ..."

She sighed, a quaint, wistful little sigh, curiously out of place, he thought, in this exquisite mouth framed only for smiles.

"I have so few real friends," she added in a whisper, so low that he thought she had not spoken, and that the elms had sighed that pathetic phrase into his ear.

"Believe me, Lady Sue, I am neither cold nor distant," he said, almost smiling now, for the situation appeared strange indeed, that this beautiful young girl, rich, courted, surrounded by an army of sycophants, should be appealing to a poor dependent for friendship. "I am only a little dazed ... as any man would be who had been dreaming ... and saw that dream vanish away. ..."

"Dreaming?"

"Yes!—we all dream sometimes you know ... and a penniless man like myself, without prospects or friends is, methinks, more prone to it than most."

"We all have dreams sometimes," she said, speaking very low, whilst her eyes sought to pierce the darkness beyond the trees. "I too ..."

She paused abruptly, and was quite still for a moment, almost holding her breath, he thought, as if she were listening. But not a sound came to disturb the silence of the woods. Blackbird and owl had ceased their fight for life, the squirrel had gone to rest: the evening air was filled only by the great murmur of the distant sea.

Cleve Court, reborn as Acol Court in Orczy's historical romance

The plot may leave something to be desired, but Orczy's ability to progress a narrative, together with some charming descriptive writing shows why she was such a popular writer in her day. Needless to say all finishes well in the end: the villain is unmasked and true love between Lady Sue and sincere Richard Lambert blossoms and triumphs. In the last sentence of the book, where Orczy could well have been referring to herself and her deeply loved husband, Montague, she says of the couple that they '….did not often stay in London. The brilliance of the Court had few attractions for them. Happiness came to them after terrible sorrows. They liked to hide it and their great love in the calm and mystery of forest-covered Thanet'.

CHAPTER NINE

CLIFF STEPS MADE THRILLING

JOHN BUCHAN

Following hard on the heels of Baroness Orczy, **John Buchan** (1875 – 1940) was another master of narrative. He also built into his thrilling stories many evocative descriptions of locations that he knew well, from Kent to Canada. He saw writing as a pleasurable pastime, a release from the stresses of his busy, career-driven life, and he liked nothing better than to take up his pen as if it were a paint brush and depict a place or a landscape to frame the action for his stories.

John Buchan

In *The Thirty-Nine Steps* (1915), Buchan's most famous story, we meet the protagonist, Richard Hannay, living in a block of flats round the corner of Buchan's real-life house at 76 Portland Place, London. Then we move on to Scotland, where Buchan grew up and spent his teenage years, and finish in Bradgate, Buchan's cleverly invented name for Broadstairs, where, with his wife and daughter, he came for a few months' rest, relaxation and recuperation in 1914.

The background to this most famous of spy stories is the German drive for power in an unstable Europe and the threat of war - and indeed the First World War actually broke out while Buchan was in Broadstairs. He paints such a memorably vivid picture of the town at the close of the novel that it is worth quoting the last chapter and *dénouement* to the story in full here. Of course, following his usual creative procedure, he fictionalizes names for the purposes of his story, and as a preliminary it is useful to check a translation key to the names of the places he recreates.

Firstly, we see Richard Hannay arriving in Bradgate, an erudite variation of Broadstairs on Buchan's part from Saxon 'brad' (= broad) and 'gaet' (= access to the sea). Another bit of erudition comes in the shape of the name of the hotel Hannay stays in, the Griffin Hotel. There were only two large seafront hotels in Broadstairs in 1914, the Albion Hotel and the Grand. The Grand was away at the far end of the main bay and would not have given the overall view as described by Buchan, whereas the Albion Hotel had, and still has, a central view out to sea and fits perfectly with Hannay's Griffin Hotel. Looking more closely, we also find that the Albion Hotel was originally called the Phoenix Hotel and was renamed the Albion Hotel in 1805 after the victorious battle of Trafalgar. With just a slight twinkle in his eye Buchan almost certainly changed one mythical winged beast, the phoenix, into another, the griffin, for his story. Looking out from a sea view room or from the terrace at the Albion Hotel one can see the famed Goodwin Sands, which made their appearance in Wilkie Collins' novel *The Fallen Leaves* (see Chapter Six), and were the dramatic centre of attention in R M Ballantyne's *The Floating Light of the Goodwin Sands* (see Chapter Seven). Buchan gives this feature the curious name, Cock sands, complete with the lightship that we met in Ballantyne's story.

Next we come to the Ruff, a big chalk headland. It is not difficult to see that this headland equates to the North Foreland area of Broadstairs, just a short walk along the coast from the Albion Hotel. The staircases cut into the cliffs, which now become important in the story and are a legacy of Broadstairs' long history of smuggling (see Chapters One and Four,) are still clearly in evidence today. The one to which Buchan attributes thirty-nine steps (in reality there were seventy-eight, which Buchan halved to give a more memorably resonant title), is the key to identifying the house and headquarters of the German Black Stone spy ring, as the entrance to this staircase is just opposite the house and marks it. The name he gives this house is Trafalgar Lodge, possibly a reference again to the Battle of Trafalgar and the re-naming of the Phoenix Hotel. In fact, this house is called St Cuby, the very house Buchan's relatives had leased for a few months in the summer of 1914, and which he got to know so well while he was staying in Broadstairs at that pivotal time.

Behind the villas on the North Foreland is a large golf course, also referenced, and the cliff road, the line of turf along the cliff top, and the bushes around the entrance to the staircase can all be seen to this day. Perhaps key aspects of Broadstairs, despite their fictionalized names, have never been so authentically and thrillingly represented in fiction as in Buchan's seminal and enduring spy story.

From *The Thirty-Nine Steps* (1915):

Chapter X.
Various Parties Converging on the Sea

A pink and blue June morning found me at Bradgate looking from the Griffin Hotel over a smooth sea to the lightship on the Cock sands which seemed the size of a bell-buoy. A couple of miles farther south and much nearer the shore a small destroyer was anchored. Scaife, MacGillivray's man, who had been in the Navy, knew the boat, and told me her name and her commander's, so I sent off a wire to Sir Walter.

After breakfast Scaife got from a house-agent a key for the gates of the staircases on the Ruff. I walked with him along the sands, and sat down in a nook of the cliffs while he investigated the half-dozen of them. I didn't want to be seen, but the place at this hour was quite deserted, and all the time I was on that beach I saw nothing but the seagulls.

It took him more than an hour to do the job, and when I saw him coming towards me, conning a bit of paper, I can tell you my heart was in my mouth. Everything depended, you see, on my guess proving right.

He read aloud the number of steps in the different stairs. "Thirty-four, thirty-five, thirty-nine, forty-two, forty-seven," and "twenty-one' where the cliffs grew lower. I almost got up and shouted.

We hurried back to the town and sent a wire to MacGillivray. I wanted half a dozen men, and I directed them to divide themselves among different specified hotels. Then Scaife set out to prospect the house at the head of the thirty-nine steps.

He came back with news that both puzzled and reassured me. The house was called Trafalgar Lodge, and belonged to an old gentleman called Appleton—a retired stockbroker, the house-agent said. Mr Appleton was there a good deal in the summer time, and was in residence now—had been for the better part of a week. Scaife could pick up very little information about him, except that he was a decent old fellow, who paid his bills regularly, and was always good for a fiver for a local charity. Then Scaife seemed to have penetrated to the back door of the house, pretending he was an agent for sewing-machines. Only three servants were kept, a cook, a parlour-maid, and a housemaid, and they were just the sort that you would find in a respectable middle-class household. The cook was not the gossiping kind, and had pretty soon shut the door in his face, but Scaife said he was positive she knew nothing. Next door there was a new house building which would give good cover for observation, and the villa on the other side was to let, and its garden was rough and shrubby.

I borrowed Scaife's telescope, and before lunch went for a walk along the Ruff. I kept well behind the rows of villas, and found a good observation point on the edge of the golf-course. There I had a view of the line of turf along the cliff top, with seats placed at intervals, and the little square plots, railed in and planted with bushes, whence the staircases descended to the beach. I saw Trafalgar Lodge very plainly, a red-brick villa with a veranda, a tennis lawn behind, and in front the ordinary seaside flower-garden full of marguerites and scraggy geraniums. There was a flagstaff from which an enormous Union Jack hung limply in the still air.

Presently I observed someone leave the house and saunter along the cliff. When I got my glasses on him I saw it was an old man, wearing white flannel trousers, a blue serge jacket, and a straw hat. He carried field-glasses and a newspaper, and sat down on one of the iron seats and began to read. Sometimes he would lay down the paper and turn his glasses on the sea. He looked for a long time at the destroyer. I watched him for half an hour, till he got up and went back to the house for his luncheon, when I returned to the hotel for mine.

I wasn't feeling very confident. This decent common-place dwelling was not what I had expected. The man might be the bald archaeologist of that horrible moorland farm, or he might not. He was exactly the kind of satisfied old bird you will find in every suburb and every holiday place. If you wanted a type of the perfectly harmless person you would probably pitch on that.

But after lunch, as I sat in the hotel porch, I perked up, for I saw the thing I had hoped for and had dreaded to miss. A yacht came up from the south and dropped anchor pretty well opposite the Ruff. She seemed about a hundred and fifty tons, and I saw she belonged to the Squadron from the white ensign. So Scaife and I went down to the harbour and hired a boatman for an afternoon's fishing.

I spent a warm and peaceful afternoon. We caught between us about twenty pounds of cod and lythe, and out in that dancing blue sea I took a cheerier view of things. Above the white cliffs of the Ruff I saw the green and red of the villas, and especially the great flagstaff of Trafalgar Lodge. About four o'clock, when we had fished enough, I made the boatman row us round the yacht, which lay like a delicate white bird, ready at a moment to flee. Scaife said she must be a fast boat for her build, and that she was pretty heavily engined.

Her name was the *Ariadne*, as I discovered from the cap of one of the men who was polishing brasswork. I spoke to him, and got an answer in the soft dialect of Essex. Another hand that came along passed me the time of day in an unmistakable English tongue. Our boatman had an argument with one of them about the weather, and for a few minutes we lay on our oars close to the starboard bow.

Then the men suddenly disregarded us and bent their heads to their work as an officer came along the deck. He was a pleasant, clean-looking young fellow, and he put a question to us about our fishing in very good English. But there could be no doubt about him. His close-cropped head and the cut of his collar and tie never came out of England.

That did something to reassure me, but as we rowed back to Bradgate my obstinate doubts would not be dismissed. The thing that worried me was the reflection that my enemies knew that I had got my knowledge from Scudder, and it was Scudder who had given me the clue to this place. If they knew that Scudder had this clue, would they not be certain to change their plans? Too much depended on their success for them to take any risks. The whole question was how much they understood about Scudder's knowledge. I had talked confidently last night about Germans always sticking to a scheme, but if they had any suspicions that I was on their track they would be fools not to cover it. I wondered if the man last night had seen that I recognized him. Somehow I did not think he had, and to that I had clung. But the whole business had never seemed so difficult as that afternoon when by all calculations I should have been rejoicing in assured success.

In the hotel I met the commander of the destroyer, to whom Scaife introduced me, and with whom I had a few words. Then I thought I would put in an hour or two watching Trafalgar Lodge.

I found a place farther up the hill, in the garden of an empty house. From there I had a full view of the court, on which two figures were having a game of tennis. One was the old man, whom I had already seen; the other was a younger fellow, wearing some club colours in the scarf round his middle. They played with tremendous zest, like two city gents who wanted hard exercise to open their pores. You couldn't conceive a more innocent spectacle. They shouted and laughed and stopped for drinks, when a maid brought out two tankards on a salver. I rubbed my eyes and asked myself if I was not the most immortal fool on earth. Mystery and darkness had hung about the men who hunted me over the Scotch moor in aeroplane and motor-car, and notably about that infernal antiquarian. It was easy enough to connect those folk with the knife that pinned Scudder to the floor, and with fell designs on the world's peace. But here were two guileless citizens taking their innocuous exercise, and soon about to go indoors to a humdrum dinner, where they would talk of market prices and the last cricket scores and the gossip of their native Surbiton.

I had been making a net to catch vultures and falcons, and lo and behold! two plump thrushes had blundered into it.

Presently a third figure arrived, a young man on a bicycle, with a bag of golf-clubs slung on his back. He strolled round to the tennis lawn and was welcomed riotously by the players. Evidently they were chaffing him, and their chaff sounded horribly English. Then the plump man, mopping his brow with a silk handkerchief, announced that he must have a tub. I heard his very words—"I've got into a proper lather," he said. "This will bring down my weight and my handicap, Bob. I'll take you on tomorrow and give you a stroke a hole." You couldn't find anything much more English than that.

They all went into the house, and left me feeling a precious idiot. I had been barking up the wrong tree this time. These men might be acting; but if they were, where was their audience? They didn't know I was sitting thirty yards off in a rhododendron. It was simply impossible to believe that these three hearty fellows were anything but what they seemed—three ordinary, game-playing, suburban Englishmen, wearisome, if you like, but sordidly innocent.

And yet there were three of them; and one was old, and one was plump, and one was lean and dark; and their house chimed in with Scudder's notes; and half a mile off was lying a steam yacht with at least one German officer. I thought of Karolides lying dead and all Europe trembling on the edge of earthquake, and the men I had left behind me in London who were waiting anxiously for the events of the next hours. There was no doubt that hell was afoot somewhere. The Black Stone had won, and if it survived this June night would bank its winnings.

There seemed only one thing to do—go forward as if I had no doubts, and if I was going to make a fool of myself to do it handsomely. Never in my life have I faced a job with greater disinclination. I would rather in my then mind have walked into a den of anarchists, each with his Browning handy, or faced a charging lion with a popgun, than enter that happy home of three cheerful

Englishmen and tell them that their game was up. How they would laugh at me!

But suddenly I remembered a thing I once heard in Rhodesia from old Peter Pienaar. I have quoted Peter already in this narrative. He was the best scout I ever knew, and before he had turned respectable he had been pretty often on the windy side of the law, when he had been wanted badly by the authorities. Peter once discussed with me the question of disguises, and he had a theory which struck me at the time. He said, barring absolute certainties like fingerprints, mere physical traits were very little use for identification if the fugitive really knew his business. He laughed at things like dyed hair and false beards and such childish follies. The only thing that mattered was what Peter called "atmosphere".

If a man could get into perfectly different surroundings from those in which he had been first observed, and—this is the important part—really play up to these surroundings and behave as if he had never been out of them, he would puzzle the cleverest detectives on earth. And he used to tell a story of how he once borrowed a black coat and went to church and shared the same hymn-book with the man that was looking for him. If that man had seen him in decent company before he would have recognized him; but he had only seen him snuffing the lights in a public-house with a revolver.

The recollection of Peter's talk gave me the first real comfort that I had had that day. Peter had been a wise old bird, and these fellows I was after were about the pick of the aviary. What if they were playing Peter's game? A fool tries to look different: a clever man looks the same and is different.

Again, there was that other maxim of Peter's which had helped me when I had been a roadman. "If you are playing a part, you will never keep it up unless you convince yourself that you are *it*." That would explain the game of tennis. Those chaps didn't need to act, they just turned a handle and passed into another life, which came as naturally to them as the first. It sounds a platitude, but Peter used to say that it was the big secret of all the famous criminals.

It was now getting on for eight o'clock, and I went back and saw Scaife to give him his instructions. I arranged with him how to place his men, and then I went for a walk, for I didn't feel up to any dinner. I went round the deserted golf-course, and then to a point on the cliffs farther north beyond the line of the villas.

On the little trim newly-made roads I met people in flannels coming back from tennis and the beach, and a coastguard from the wireless station, and donkeys and pierrots padding homewards. Out at sea in the blue dusk I saw lights appear on the *Ariadne* and on the destroyer away to the south, and beyond the Cock sands the bigger lights of steamers making for the Thames. The whole scene was so peaceful and ordinary that I got more dashed in spirits every second. It took all my resolution to stroll towards Trafalgar Lodge about half-past nine.

On the way I got a piece of solid comfort from the sight of a greyhound that was swinging along at a nursemaid's heels. He reminded me of a dog I used to have in Rhodesia, and of the time when I took him hunting with me in the Pali hills. We were after rhebok, the dun kind, and I recollected how we had followed one beast, and both he and I had clean lost it. A greyhound works by sight, and my eyes are good enough, but that buck simply leaked out of the landscape. Afterwards I found out how it managed it. Against the grey rock of the kopjes it showed no more than a crow against a thundercloud. It didn't need to run away; all it had to do was to stand still and melt into the background.

Suddenly as these memories chased across my brain I thought of my present case and applied the moral. The Black Stone didn't need to bolt. They were quietly absorbed into the landscape. I was on the right track, and I jammed that down in my mind and vowed never to forget it. The last word was with Peter Pienaar.

Scaife's men would be posted now, but there was no sign of a soul. The house stood as open as a market-place for anybody to observe. A three-foot railing separated it from the cliff road; the windows on the ground-floor were all open, and shaded lights and the low sound of voices revealed where the occupants were finishing dinner. Everything was as public and above-board as a charity bazaar. Feeling the greatest fool on earth, I opened the gate and rang the bell.

A man of my sort, who has travelled about the world in rough places, gets on perfectly well with two classes, what you may call the upper and the lower. He understands them and they understand him. I was at home with herds and tramps and roadmen, and I was sufficiently at my ease with people like Sir Walter and the men I had met the night before. I can't explain why, but it is a fact. But what fellows like me don't understand is the great comfortable, satisfied middle-class world, the folk that live in villas and suburbs. He doesn't know how they look at things, he doesn't understand their conventions, and he is as shy of them as of a black mamba. When a trim parlour-maid opened the door, I could hardly find my voice.

I asked for Mr Appleton, and was ushered in. My plan had been to walk straight into the dining-room, and by a sudden appearance wake in the men that start of recognition which would confirm my theory. But when I found myself in that neat hall the place mastered me. There were the golf-clubs and tennis-rackets, the straw hats and caps, the rows of gloves, the sheaf of walking-sticks, which you will find in ten thousand British homes. A stack of neatly folded coats and waterproofs covered the top of an old oak chest; there was a grandfather clock ticking; and some polished brass warming-pans on the walls, and a barometer, and a print of Chiltern winning the St Leger. The place was as orthodox as an Anglican church. When the maid asked me for my name I gave it automatically, and was shown into the smoking-room, on the right side of the hall.

That room was even worse. I hadn't time to examine it, but I could see some framed group photographs above the mantelpiece, and I could have sworn they were English public school or college. I had only one glance, for I managed to pull myself together and go after the maid. But I was too late. She had already entered the dining-room and given my name to her master, and I had missed the chance of seeing how the three took it.

When I walked into the room the old man at the head of the table had risen and turned round to meet me. He was in evening dress—a short coat and black tie, as was the other, whom I called in my own mind the plump one. The third, the dark fellow, wore a blue serge suit and a soft white collar, and the colours of some club or school.

The old man's manner was perfect. "Mr Hannay?" he said hesitatingly. "Did you wish to see me? One moment, you fellows, and I'll rejoin you. We had better go to the smoking-room."

Though I hadn't an ounce of confidence in me, I forced myself to play the game. I pulled up a chair and sat down on it.

"I think we have met before," I said, "and I guess you know my business."

The light in the room was dim, but so far as I could see their faces, they played the part of mystification very well.

"Maybe, maybe," said the old man. "I haven't a very good memory, but I'm afraid you must tell me your errand, sir, for I really don't know it."

"Well, then," I said, and all the time I seemed to myself to be talking pure foolishness—"I have come to tell you that the game's up. I have a warrant for the arrest of you three gentlemen."

"Arrest," said the old man, and he looked really shocked. "Arrest! Good God, what for?"

"For the murder of Franklin Scudder in London on the 23rd day of last month."

"I never heard the name before," said the old man in a dazed voice.

One of the others spoke up. "That was the Portland Place murder. I read about it. Good heavens, you must be mad, sir! Where do you come from?"

"Scotland Yard," I said.

After that for a minute there was utter silence. The old man was staring at his plate and fumbling with a nut, the very model of innocent bewilderment.

Then the plump one spoke up. He stammered a little, like a man picking his words.

"Don't get flustered, uncle," he said. "It is all a ridiculous mistake; but these things happen sometimes, and we can easily set it right. It won't be hard to prove our innocence. I can show that I was out of the country on the 23rd of May, and Bob was in a nursing home. You were in London, but you can explain what you were doing."

"Right, Percy! Of course that's easy enough. The 23rd! That was the day after Agatha's wedding. Let me see. What was I doing? I came up in the morning from Woking, and lunched at the club with Charlie Symons. Then—oh yes, I dined with the Fishmongers. I remember, for the punch didn't agree with me, and I was seedy next morning. Hang it all, there's the cigar-box I brought back from the dinner." He pointed to an object on the table, and laughed nervously.

"I think, sir," said the young man, addressing me respectfully, "you will see you are mistaken. We want to assist the law like all Englishmen, and we don't want Scotland Yard to be making fools of themselves. That's so, uncle?"

"Certainly, Bob." The old fellow seemed to be recovering his voice. "Certainly, we'll do anything in our power to assist the authorities. But—but this is a bit too much. I can't get over it."

"How Nellie will chuckle," said the plump man. "She always said that you would die of boredom because nothing ever happened to you. And now you've got it thick and strong," and he began to laugh very pleasantly.

"By Jove, yes. Just think of it! What a story to tell at the club. Really, Mr Hannay, I suppose I should be angry, to show my innocence, but it's too funny! I almost forgive you the fright you gave me! You looked so glum, I thought I might have been walking in my sleep and killing people."

It couldn't be acting, it was too confoundedly genuine. My heart went into my boots, and my first impulse was to apologize and clear out. But I told myself I must see it through, even though I was to be the laughing-stock of Britain. The light from the dinner-table candlesticks was not very good, and to cover my confusion I got up, walked to the door and switched on the electric light. The sudden glare made them blink, and I stood scanning the three faces.

Well, I made nothing of it. One was old and bald, one was stout, one was dark and thin. There was nothing in their appearance to prevent them being the three who had hunted me in Scotland, but there was nothing to identify them. I simply can't explain why I who, as a roadman, had looked into two pairs of eyes, and as Ned Ainslie into another pair, why I, who have a good memory and reasonable powers of observation, could find no satisfaction. They seemed exactly what they professed to be, and I could not have sworn to one of them.

There in that pleasant dining-room, with etchings on the walls, and a picture of an old lady in a bib above the mantelpiece, I could see nothing to connect them with the moorland desperadoes. There was a silver cigarette-box beside me, and I saw that it had been won by Percival Appleton, Esq., of the St Bede's Club, in a golf tournament. I had to keep a firm hold of Peter Pienaar to prevent myself bolting out of that house.

"Well," said the old man politely, "are you reassured by your scrutiny, sir?"

I couldn't find a word.

"I hope you'll find it consistent with your duty to drop this ridiculous business. I make no complaint, but you'll see how annoying it must be to respectable people."

I shook my head.

"O Lord," said the young man. "This is a bit too thick!"

"Do you propose to march us off to the police station?" asked the plump one. "That might be the best way out of it, but I suppose you won't be content with the local branch. I have the right to ask to see your warrant, but I don't wish to cast any aspersions upon you. You are only doing your duty. But you'll admit it's horribly awkward. What do you propose to do?"

There was nothing to do except to call in my men and have them arrested, or to confess my blunder and clear out. I felt mesmerized by the whole place, by the air of obvious innocence—not innocence merely, but frank honest bewilderment and concern in the three faces.

"Oh, Peter Pienaar," I groaned inwardly, and for a moment I was very near damning myself for a fool and asking their pardon.

"Meantime I vote we have a game of bridge," said the plump one. "It will give Mr Hannay time to think over things, and you know we have been wanting a fourth player. Do you play, sir?"

I accepted as if it had been an ordinary invitation at the club. The whole business had mesmerized me. We went into the smoking-room where a card-table was set out, and I was offered things to smoke and drink. I took my place at the table in a kind of dream. The window was open and the moon was flooding the cliffs and sea with a great tide of yellow light. There was moonshine, too, in my head. The three had recovered their composure, and were talking easily—just the kind of slangy talk you will hear in any golf club-house. I must have cut a rum figure, sitting there knitting my brows with my eyes wandering.

My partner was the young dark one. I play a fair hand at bridge, but I must have been rank bad that night. They saw that they had got me puzzled, and that put them more than ever at their ease. I kept looking at their faces, but they conveyed nothing to me. It was not that they looked different; they *were* different. I clung desperately to the words of Peter Pienaar.

Then something awoke me.

The old man laid down his hand to light a cigar. He didn't pick it up at once, but sat back for a moment in his chair, with his fingers tapping on his knees.

It was the movement I remembered when I had stood before him in the moorland farm, with the pistols of his servants behind me.

A little thing, lasting only a second, and the odds were a thousand to one that I might have had my eyes on my cards at the time and missed it. But I didn't, and, in a flash, the air seemed to clear. Some shadow lifted from my brain, and I was looking at the three men with full and absolute recognition.

The clock on the mantelpiece struck ten o'clock.

The three faces seemed to change before my eyes and reveal their secrets. The young one was the murderer. Now I saw cruelty and ruthlessness, where before I had only seen good-humour. His knife, I made certain, had skewered Scudder to the floor. His kind had put the bullet in Karolides.

The plump man's features seemed to dislimn, and form again, as I looked at them. He hadn't a face, only a hundred masks that he could assume when he pleased. That chap must have been a superb actor. Perhaps he had been Lord Alloa of the night before; perhaps not; it didn't matter. I wondered if he was the fellow who had first tracked Scudder, and left his card on him. Scudder had said he lisped, and I could imagine how the adoption of a lisp might add terror.

But the old man was the pick of the lot. He was sheer brain, icy, cool, calculating, as ruthless as a steam hammer. Now that my eyes were opened I wondered where I had seen the benevolence. His jaw was like chilled steel, and his eyes had the inhuman luminosity of a bird's. I went on playing, and every second a greater hate welled up in my heart. It almost choked me, and I couldn't answer when my partner spoke. Only a little longer could I endure their company.

"Whew! Bob! Look at the time," said the old man. "You'd better think about catching your train. Bob's got to go to town tonight," he added, turning to me. The voice rang now as false as hell. I looked at the clock, and it was nearly half-past ten.

"I am afraid he must put off his journey," I said.

"Oh, damn," said the young man. "I thought you had dropped that rot. I've simply got to go. You can have my address, and I'll give any security you like."

"No," I said, "you must stay."

At that I think they must have realized that the game was desperate. Their only chance had been to convince me that I was playing the fool, and that had failed. But the old man spoke again.

"I'll go bail for my nephew. That ought to content you, Mr Hannay." Was it fancy, or did I detect some halt in the smoothness of that voice?

There must have been, for as I glanced at him, his eyelids fell in that hawk-like hood which fear had stamped on my memory.

I blew my whistle.

In an instant the lights were out. A pair of strong arms gripped me round the waist, covering the pockets in which a man might be expected to carry a pistol.

"*Schnell, Franz,*' cried a voice, "*das Boot, das Boot!*" As it spoke I saw two of my fellows emerge on the moonlit lawn.

The young dark man leapt for the window, was through it, and over the low fence before a hand could touch him. I grappled the old chap, and the room seemed to fill with figures. I saw the plump one collared, but my eyes were all for the out-of-doors, where Franz sped on over the road towards the railed entrance to the beach stairs. One man followed him, but he had no chance. The gate of the stairs locked behind the fugitive, and I stood staring, with my hands on the old boy's throat, for such a time as a man might take to descend those steps to the sea.

Suddenly my prisoner broke from me and flung himself on the wall. There was a click as if a lever had been pulled. Then came a low rumbling far, far below the ground, and through the window I saw a cloud of chalky dust pouring out of the shaft of the stairway.

Someone switched on the light.

The old man was looking at me with blazing eyes.

"He is safe," he cried. "You cannot follow in time.... He is gone.... He has triumphed.... *Der Schwarze Stein ist in der Siegeskrone.*"

There was more in those eyes than any common triumph. They had been hooded like a bird of prey, and now they flamed with a hawk's pride. A white fanatic heat burned in them, and I realized for the first time the terrible thing I had been up against. This man was more than a spy; in his foul way he had been a patriot.

As the handcuffs clinked on his wrists I said my last word to him.

"I hope Franz will bear his triumph well. I ought to tell you that the *Ariadne* for the last hour has been in our hands."

Seven weeks later, as all the world knows, we went to war. I joined the New Army the first week, and owing to my Matabele experience got a captain's commission straight off. But I had done my best service, I think, before I put on khaki.

St Cuby, or 'Trafalgar Lodge'

The Albion Hotel, or the 'Griffin Hotel'

The cliff road, with bushes around the entrance to the steps and line of turf along the cliff top. The road follows round to the golf course nearby.

'the railed entrance to the beach stairs'

As with Charles Dickens, where the town inspired the author and the author ended up inspiring the town, so with John Buchan. Right next to the Charles Dickens pub is the Thirty-Nine Steps Brewhouse; there is a Thirty-Nine Steps town trail suggested by the John Buchan Society; and one year the local council even felt moved to organize a John Buchan day. Any number of articles and sections in local history books, and leaflets on the town's connection with the novel, have brought so many interested parties converging on the 'high-toned' North Foreland Estate, where the residents 'like to keep by themselves' (see Chapter IX of the novel), that the present day residents have recently felt it necessary to install a heavy, securely locked gate at the top and bottom of the steps that might have deterred even the German spy Franz. Buchan's short but brilliant novel, adapted so many times for film and theatre, and known throughout the world, has become an integral part of the Broadstairs story.

CHAPTER TEN

SEASIDE COMEDY

GEORGE AND WHEEDON GROSSMITH

The **Grossmith** brothers, George (1847 – 1912) and Wheedon (1854 – 1919), take us to a world far removed from John Buchan's spies, suspense and high drama. Here the curtain now swings delightfully open on comedy. In the brothers' *The Diary of a Nobody* (1892) the lower middle-class life with pretensions of the Pooter family is depicted in richly comic detail, throwing an amusingly unforgiving light on their petty snobberies, trifling concerns and underwhelming ambitions.

George Grossmith   **Wheedon Grossmith**

We meet Charles Pooter, a City of London clerk, his wife Caroline (Carrie) and learn about their feckless son William, who prefers to be called by his middle name, Lupin, which he considers more elevated – an oblique reference here perhaps to Dickens' *The Tuggses at Ramsgate*, where the son gentrifies his name from Simon to Cymon (see Chapter Five).

The narrative arises out of the diary that the self-regarding Charles Pooter keeps, with the book starting off as they settle into their new home, 'The Laurels', in the desirable London suburb of Holloway. From mixed reviews when it first appeared, *The Diary of a Nobody* came to be considered as something of a comic masterpiece and a great satire on late Victorian society. It influenced a great number of subsequent writers, from Evelyn Waugh, who thought it 'the funniest book in the world', to, in our day, Sue Townsend and her *The Secret Diary of Adrian Mole Aged 13¾*, as well as Helen Fielding in her *Bridget Jones' Diary*. It is also hard not to mention the *Private Eye* satire of the 1990s, *The Secret Diary of John Major Aged 47¾*, which referenced John Major's lower middle-class origins à la Charles Pooter as well as the Sue Townsend book.

Here Charles and Carrie discuss where they will take their annual holiday week and decide on Broadstairs. Their son Lupin, who was working in Oldham as a bank clerk, has been dismissed for idleness and so he comes to join his parents on their holiday. We then fast forward to their stay in Broadstairs and while there also meet their friends, the Cummingses and the Gowings, who are holidaying nearby.

From *The Diary of a Nobody* (1892):

> July 31.—Carrie was very pleased with the bangle, which I left with an affectionate note on her dressing-table last night before going to bed. I told Carrie we should have to start for our holiday next Saturday. She replied quite happily that she did not mind, except that the weather was so bad, and she feared that Miss Jibbons would not be able to get her a seaside dress in time. I told Carrie that I thought the drab one with pink bows looked quite good enough; and Carrie said she should not think of wearing it. I was about to discuss the matter, when, remembering the argument yesterday, resolved to hold my tongue.
>
> I said to Carrie: "I don't think we can do better than 'Good old Broadstairs.'" Carrie not only, to my astonishment, raised an objection to Broadstairs, for the first time; but begged me not to use the expression, "Good old," but to leave it to Mr. Stillbrook and other *gentlemen* of his type. Hearing my 'bus pass the window, I was obliged to rush out of the house without kissing Carrie as usual; and I shouted to her: "I leave it to you to decide." On returning in the evening, Carrie said she thought as the time was so short she had decided on Broadstairs, and had written to Mrs. Beck, Harbour View Terrace, for apartments.

August 2.—Mrs. Beck wrote to say we could have our usual rooms at Broadstairs. That's off our mind. Bought a coloured shirt and a pair of tan-coloured boots, which I see many of the swell clerks wearing in the City, and hear are all the "go."

August 11.—Although it is a serious matter having our boy Lupin on our hands, still it is satisfactory to know he was asked to resign from the Bank simply because "he took no interest in his work, and always arrived an hour (sometimes two hours) late." We can all start off on Monday to Broadstairs with a light heart. This will take my mind off the worry of the last few days, which have been wasted over a useless correspondence with the manager of the Bank at Oldham.

August 13.—Hurrah! at Broadstairs. Very nice apartments near the station. On the cliffs they would have been double the price. The landlady had a nice five o'clock dinner and tea ready, which we all enjoyed, though Lupin seemed fastidious because there happened to be a fly in the butter. It was very wet in the evening, for which I was thankful, as it was a good excuse for going to bed early. Lupin said he would sit up and read a bit.

August 20.—I am glad our last day at the seaside was fine, though clouded overhead. We went over to Cummings' (at Margate) in the evening, and as it was cold, we stayed in and played games; Gowing, as usual, overstepping the mark. He suggested we should play "Cutlets," a game we never heard of. He sat on a chair, and asked Carrie to sit on his lap, an invitation which dear Carrie rightly declined. After some species of wrangling, I sat on Gowing's knees and Carrie sat on the edge of mine. Lupin sat on the edge of Carrie's lap, then Cummings on Lupin's, and Mrs. Cummings on her husband's. We looked very ridiculous, and laughed a good deal. Gowing then said: "Are you a believer in the Great Mogul?" We had to answer all together: "Yes—oh, yes!" (three times). Gowing said: "So am I," and suddenly got up. The result of this stupid joke was that we all fell on the ground, and poor Carrie banged her head against the corner of the fender. Mrs. Cummings put some vinegar on; but through this we missed the last train, and had to drive back to Broadstairs, which cost me seven-and-sixpence.

Charles Pooter (left) and Lupin in Broadstairs, illustration by Wheedon Grossmith

Wheedon Grossmith, as well as co-authoring the book with his brother George, produced all the illustrations - witness his Broadstairs drawing above. Having trained as an artist, but not having that extra talent needed to achieve great success, he, like Baroness Orczy (see Chapter Eight), turned his hand to writing, while clearly enjoying the opportunity to display his artistic skill. In much the same way George, having started life as an actor, found that he could do better as a writer. The two of them certainly discovered their voice in *The Diary of a Nobody* and, in an incidental way as seen in this extract, confirmed how popular Broadstairs had become as a suitable holiday destination for Londoners. The book has never been out of print since it first appeared, and Broadstairs has never ceased to attract Londoners.

FRANK RICHARDS

Frank Richards (1876 – 1961), creator of that famous comic schoolboy Billy Bunter, located his equally famous public school called Greyfriars, the setting for his Bunter stories, somewhere in Kent. But the school's vague siting meant that it could never be pinned down conclusively to one actual spot, in spite of a sketch map in one story of the weekly boys' periodical *The Magnet* suggesting somewhere west of Dover. No doubt the location of Bunter's school lay mainly in the topography of Richards' imagination, but there are indications that he often had the Isle of Thanet in mind.

Frank Richards

Billy Bunter as depicted by *The Magnet* artist C. H. Chapman

In the mid-1920s Frank Richards, whose real name was Charles Hamilton (Frank Richards was one of his very many pseudonyms), moved to the Kingsgate area of Broadstairs. This move coincided with a change of emphasis in the Greyfriars stories. The school had first appeared in *The Magnet* in 1908 and Billy Bunter was initially only a minor character among the other schoolboys portrayed, such as Harry Wharton and Bob Cherry. But it was after

Richards came to live in Thanet that he began to realize the full comic potential of Billy Bunter, moving the 'Fat Owl of the Remove' firmly to centre stage. Although the reclusive Richards lived mainly in the world of his imagination, he liked to walk, got to know his surroundings very well and inevitably started to use features of the locality in his descriptions of the area around Greyfriars.

Scenes around Greyfriars

As examples, he describes the cliff path that led from Greyfriars to Cliff House Girls' School, which could well have been the cliff path at the end of Percy Avenue, the road where Richards lived. An episode where Bunter is rescued from the waves would appear to derive from a real rescue scene witnessed by Richards in Kingsgate's Botany Bay. Also, Pegg Bay next to Greyfriars very probably owes its name to Pegwell Bay next to Ramsgate.

It is in the seaside resort of Pegg Bay, which appears to be modelled on Ramsate itself rather than the smaller, beach-less Pegwell Bay adjacent to it, that we meet Bunter in the following extract. The background to the story is that Bunter's identical cousin, Wally, is staying in Pegg, and Bunter has persuaded his cousin to change places with him so that he can lounge around on the Pegg Bay beach.

From *Billy Bunter's Double* (1955):

CAUGHT!

"BUNTER!"
"Oh!" gasped Billy Bunter.
He nearly swallowed a cigarette.

Billy Bunter hadn't expected to see Prout. He had forgotten the portly existence of the master of the Fifth Form at Greyfriars. Prout happened like a bolt from the blue.

A moment earlier, Bunter had been enjoying life.

In term time, lessons were a pest that no fellow at school could hope to escape. But Bunter was escaping them. So long as he could, so to speak, go on playing a substitute in the field, he could go on escaping them. Minus Wally, he would have been grinding Latin with Quelch, or maths with Lascelles, or French with Mossoo, or rolling reluctantly down to games-practice, or dodging Coker of the Fifth. Plus Wally, he was able to sun himself on the beach, stroll on the promenade: sprawl on the sands like a fat lizard: and generally indulge in laziness to his fat heart's content. It was a change in Bunter's opinion, very much for the better.

Why Wally preferred Greyfriars to the joys of the seaside, was a mystery to Billy Bunter: but Wally did, and the fat Owl was only too willing to let him have all the Latin, maths, French, and games-practice that he wanted. He would have been glad to carry on this peculiar game of changed identity right up to the end of the term, had it been possible.

Moreover, Billy Bunter was not, for once, in his accustomed "stony" state. He had cash to jingle in his pockets.

He had pointed out that Wally was getting a "holiday with pay": so if he, Billy, was to have the holiday instead of Wally, it was only fair that he should have the pay also!

Wally had not quite seemed to see that. But when they parted, a couple of Wally's pound notes had been left with Billy. So, for the moment, the fat Owl was unusually affluent.

It was like Billy Bunter to "spread" himself, when he was in funds, and the eye of authority was not upon him. Hence the cigarette sticking out of the largest mouth in Pegg when Prout happened.

Billy Bunter fancied, or fancied that he fancied, a smoke! Why not, when he was his own master, clear of beaks, clear of prefects, free to do what he jolly well liked? So the Owl of the Remove had invested a spot of Wally's cash in a packet of cigarettes.

Now he was sitting on the soft sand, his plump back against a rock, his little fat legs stretched out in lazy comfort: blinking through his big spectacles at the sea, the boats, the trippers, the bathers, smoking a cigarette and determined to believe that he liked it. Prout was no more in his thoughts than the man in the moon.

But it was Prout that happened.

Really there was nothing surprising in a Greyfriars master taking a walk by the sea after class, if Bunter had thought of it. Prout, portly and pompous, rolled on his way rather like a stately Spanish galleon, with a benevolent eye for common mortals crowding the beach. But the benevolence faded out of his portly face at the sight of a Greyfriars junior sitting against the rock smoking a cigarette.

Prout stared. Then he glared. Then he changed course, and bore down on Billy Bunter, with a frown on his portly brow. And as an extensive shadow fell between him and the sunshine, and a well-known voice boomed "Bunter!", the startled fat Owl gave a jump like a startled rabbit, blinked up at Prout, and gasped.

He forgot the cigarette for a moment. But the next moment he was reminded of it, as it slipped into his mouth.

The hot end of that cigarette was very hot.

"Wow!" roared Bunter. It was doubtful whether Bunter had really been enjoying that cigarette before. Assuredly he was not enjoying it now.

"Ow! Ooooh! Oh! Wow!" He spluttered that cigarette out of his mouth, and spluttered and spluttered. "Oooooogh! I'm burnt! Woooh!'

"Bunter!" boomed Prout, heartlessly indifferent to the fat Owl's anguish. "Bunter! What does this mean?"

"Oooooooogh!"

Bunter rubbed his mouth frantically. From the bottom of his fat heart he wished that he had not indulged that fancy for a smoke!

"I find you here. You are well aware, Bunter, that Pegg is outside school bounds, except on half-holidays. Yet I find you here!"

"Urrrrrghh!"

"And smoking-smoking a cigarette-."

"Wurrrggh!"

"You have changed your clothes - you are not even wearing a school cap! What does this mean, Bunter?"

"I-I-I-oooogh!" Billy Bunter, recovering a little from the hot end of the cigarette, blinked up at the portly Fifth-form master in dismay. He was fairly caught! He had a terrifying vision of Prout marching him back to the school, to hand him over to Quelch - with a Bunter already there! Two Bunters on one spot meant the whole scheme coming to pieces.

"I shall take you to your form-master! He will deal with you!" said Prout, sternly. "Get on your feet at once, Bunter! Do you hear me? You will explain to Mr. Quelch the meaning of this Bunter! Smoking - Pah!"

"Oh, lor'!' I-I ain't Bunter, sir!" gasped the fat Owl, desperately. It was his last resource.

Billy Bunter did not want to make it known that a relative so closely resembling himself had come to stay at Pegg. That was a circumstance which, in the other circumstances, it was much wiser to keep dark, very dark indeed. But anything was better than being marched back to the school, to astonish Greyfriars with the unexpected sight of two Bunters at once!

"What?" boomed Prout.

"I-I ain't, really, sir!" stuttered the dismayed fat Owl.

"I'm my cousin, sir-."

"Wha-a-at?"

"I-I am really, sir! We - we're much alike, sir," burbled Bunter. "We - we've often been taken for one another, sir! I-I-I'm not me at all-."

"Bless my soul!" ejaculated Mr. Prout, gazing at the fat Owl. "Bunter, I doubt whether you are in your right senses-."

"But I-I ain't Bunter, sir, I'm my cousin Wally-!" gasped the fat Owl. "I-I assure you, sir, that I ain't me at all, but-but another chap, sir! I-I've never seen you before, sir! I-I don't even know you're Mr. Prout, Sir! I-I-I-. Wow! Ow!"

Prout stooped, grasped a collar, and jerked the fat Owl to his feet.

"Now come with me!" he rapped. "Oh, lor'!"

Bunter came. He had no choice about that. In utter dismay, he rolled along by the side of the Fifth-form master. He wondered dizzily whether Prout, if he had come upon the real Wally in Pegg, would have collared him like this! No doubt Wally would have been able to convince Prout of his mistake. But Billy's fat wits were not equal to such an emergency. Somehow, he had failed to convince Prout that he was not himself but somebody else!

As they came up from the beach to the promenade, Bunter lagged behind, hoping for a chance to dodge away. An eye glittered round at him.

"Bunter!"

"Oh! I-I wasn't going to cut, sir-."

"Come!"

Bunter rolled on dismally. And as Greyfriars drew nearer and nearer, Billy Bunter's fat heart sank lower and lower, till it seemed almost to be sinking into Wally's tan shoes.

Such a passage shows how Greyfriars could easily have gravitated to Thanet in Richards' mind, perhaps joining the many independent schools that existed in the area at that time. For the man who spent every day of his long life writing stories for young people, with settings for adventures ranging from America to Africa, totalling a lifetime output of around one hundred million words, more than any other author in the world, everything was imagined and everything was imaginable.

Even the invented name Frank Richards became more real to the man than his actual name, Charles Hamilton, as illustrated by the fact that he called his autobiography *The Autobiography of Frank Richards*. In this imaginary world his schoolboy chums never grew old. As George Orwell remarked in 1940, nothing ever changes in the stories, no-one grows up and Bunter is always in the Remove. Likewise Frank Richards himself never seemed to grow old. As his much-loved niece, Una Hamilton Wright, later commented, he always gave the impression of being young right up to the end of his life. Physically, he lived on the Isle of Thanet for thirty-five years until his death in 1961. But mentally he lived on an isle of eternal youth.

CHAPTER ELEVEN

SEEN FROM THE AIR

DENNIS WHEATLEY

At the grave of **Dennis Wheatley** (1897 – 1977) in Brookwood Cemetery, Surrey, we read a small but powerful inscription proclaiming the incumbent's place among the stars: 'Prince of Thrillers'. With this highest-of-earning writers, whose popular fiction was globally famous during a good half of the twentieth century, we have left comedy far behind and are firmly back in the territory of suspense and adventure, with a heavy dose of the occult thrown in.

Dennis Wheatley

Dennis Wheatley's weird and wonderful thrillers, in spite their often implausible plots and somewhat shaky writing style, had one particular strength in common. Their background was meticulously researched and the locations they ranged across were wonderfully and authentically evoked. Thanks to his love of travel, first sparked off in his geography classes at Skelsmergh House School in Margate when he was a boy, Wheatley was able to set his thrillers convincingly in countries as different and as far apart as Sri Lanka and Egypt, Greece and Mexico, or Russia and Spain. And he certainly knew a good location when he saw one.

This sense of place also applied nearer to home, and never more so than when it came to choosing the Isle of Thanet as the setting for his 1930s thriller *Contraband*. Londoner

Wheatley always retained fond memories of Thanet thanks to his happy time as a boarding pupil in the junior section of Skelsmergh House School, headed by the enlightened pedagogue G N Hester. He got to know the area well, and was particularly fascinated by the collection of stuffed wild animals from Africa mounted in galleries at Quex House in Birchington.

Quex House is a fine manor house, set in two hundred and fifty acres of parkland and gardens, and Wheatley became well acquainted with it during his school holidays. This came about because his paternal grandfather, also called Dennis Wheatley, having retired to a part of Westgate bordering on Birchington, knew the head gardener at Quex, and Wheatley often stayed with his grandparents in vacation time. He loved to hear the exploits of the owner, Major Percy Powell-Cotton, who had hunted game in Africa and shipped back many of the animals. Later in life, after success had come, Wheatley determined that Quex House and Park would make another great location for a story. He eagerly met the elderly Major Powell-Cotton on a visit to Thanet and asked him if he could use Quex House and Park by name in a story. The major, who Wheatley immediately elevated to the rank of Colonel, agreed.

In the story Wheatley finally wrote, Quex House becomes the headquarters of a smuggling gang engaged in importing foreign terrorists and weapons into Britain, with the aim of destabilizing the government and the country. The mastermind of this devilish plan is the power-mad dwarf Lord Gavin Fortescue, and it falls upon Wheatley's hero, the tough, cynical, snobbish Gregory Sallust, prototype of James Bond, to defeat him. In the process we see a lot of small planes buzzing around over Thanet. The smugglers are constantly landing and taking off from the lawns in Quex Park under cover of night and we see Sallust, no mean pilot himself, flying around East Kent in pursuit of the smugglers. In this mission Sallust is supporting the man in charge of the investigation into the smuggling operation, Inspector Gerry Wells, who also takes to the air in his own light aircraft. Here we meet the inspector as, somewhat beyond the call of duty, he invites a young lady staying at Quex House for a spin over Thanet. The young person in question is called Milly, who has been looked after by the caretaker of Quex House, Mrs Bird, since her father died.

Quex House and Park, with its ample lawns

From *Contraband* (1936):

Inspector Gerry Wells dropped off at Birchington churchyard in which Dante Gabriel Rossetti lies buried, but he did not pause to visit the poet's grave. Instead he turned up Park Lane; his thoughts very much with the living. Outside the west gate of Quex Park he met his man who was keeping in touch with Mrs. Bird.

"Anything fresh, Thompson?" he asked.

"No, sir, nothing. There've been no more visitors since you left last night, and Mrs. Bird tells me the lady who came down by car slept in the place. She's still there as far as I know."

Wells nodded and walked on up the wooded driveway then, skirting the back of the museum, he reached the side entrance to the house.

Mrs. Bird appeared from the kitchen garden with a basket full of runner beans just as he reached the door, and she confirmed Thompson's report.

"When the foreign lady turned up she had her bit of supper," she said, "and told me she meant to stay the night. I always keep a couple of bedrooms ready because that's his lordship's orders. After her meal she went straight up without a word except that I wasn't to call her until she rang for breakfast."

Milly came out at that moment and smiled shyly at the Inspector. He nodded to her cheerfully.

"We're on the right track now, but it's a matter of waiting until midday, or rather until Mr Sallust turns up again and I doubt if he'll be here much before then. I've got to kick my heels around for the next few hours and so I was wondering…."

"Wondering what?" Milly asked him.

"Well, my plane's at Manston aerodrome, only a couple of miles away and I was wondering if you meant what you said about liking to come up for a flip some time."

Milly paled a little under her creamy skin. "I – I think it would be rather fun – with you."

"You don't mind, Mrs. Bird?' he asked the older woman.

"As long as you bring her back safe I don't, but aeroplanes are tricky things, aren't they?"

"Not if they're looked after properly. Night landings in unknown country aren't much fun, but it's no more risky than going for a ride in a car on a lovely day like this."

"All right, I'll get my hat." Milly turned away, but he stopped her.

"You don't need that – only get it blown off as mine's an open plane. I'll borrow a leather jacket for you from one of the pilots."

Milly looked at Mrs. Bird. "You're sure you don't mind, Aunty?"

"Of course I don't, my pet, as long as you take care. Run along now and enjoy yourself."

Gerry and the girl left the back of the house and made their way by the side path through the shrubbery out on to the east drive. Both were silent for a few minutes, racking their brains for a subject of conversation. Then Gerry glanced towards the old tower which rose out of a coppice some hundred yards away to their right with the steel structure on its top, which looked like a miniature Eiffel Tower and could be seen above the tree-tops of the park for many miles in all directions.

"What's that place?" he asked. "Apart, I mean, from the fact that they may use it now as a signal station to guide their planes in."

"It's called the Waterloo tower, I think," she said, "built in the year of the battle you know, and it has a peal of bells, twelve of them, the finest in Kent up to a few years ago. Canterbury Cathedral had only ten, until they added another couple and came equal with this lot here. There's another tower over there too," she glanced towards their left where a tall brick building crowned a low fenced-in mound that rose from the grass land. "The old gardener told me that major Powell-Cotton's father was awfully keen on ships and things; so he used to signal from it to his friends in the navy when they sailed across the bay. The sea is hidden from us here by the trees but it's only a mile away."

"I see he made a collection of old cannons too," Wells remarked, looking at the six-deep semi-circle of ancient guns which occupied the mound.

"That's right. Some of them came from the Royal George, I'm told and the little baby ones were taken from Kingsgate Castle. The mound itself is an old Saxon burial ground, raised in honour of some great chief, and it's supposed to be the reason we have a ghost here. She's called the White Lady and walks along a path through the woods behind the tower at night until she reaches the mound, then she disappears. They say she's the chief's young wife and she haunts the place where he was buried."

"Ever seen her?"

"No, and I don't think anyone has for a long time now; all the same I wouldn't walk along that path at night for anything."

"Not if I were with you?" Gerry asked, smiling at her.

She blushed a little. "Well, I might then – that would be different."

A few moments later they reached the park gates and took the by-roads through the open cornfields towards Manston. They were silent for a good portion of their two-mile walk but strangely happy in each other's company.

At the aerodrome a friendly artificer lent Milly a flying coat and she was soon installed in the observer's seat of Wells's Tiger Moth, a little scared, but even more excited at starting on her first flight.

For nearly an hour they cruised over eastern Kent, first along the northern shore over Birchington, Herne Bay and Whitstable, then south-east to Canterbury, where the towers of the ancient cathedral, lifting high above the twisting streets of the town, were thrown up by the strong sunlight which patterned the stonework like delicate lace against the black shadows made by its embrasures. Ten minutes later they had reached the coast again and were circling over Hythe on the southern shore of the county. Turning east they visited Sandgate, Folkestone and Dover, flying low round the tower of the old castle upon its cliff, while below them the cross-channel steamers and the destroyers in the Admiralty basin looked like toy ships that one could pick up in the hand and push out with a stick upon a voyage across a pond. Away over the Channel the white cliffs of Calais showed faintly in the summer haze. From Dover they sailed on to Walmer, Deal and Sandwich, then across Pegwell Bay to Ramsgate, and completed the circle of the Thanet coast by passing low over the long beaches of Broadstairs, Margate and Westgate, where the holiday crowd swarmed like black ants in their thousands and countless white faces stared up towards the roaring plane, waving hands and handkerchiefs in salutation as it soared low overhead.

"Well, how did you like it?" Gerry Wells turned to glance over his shoulder as he brought the plane to a halt once more on the Manston landing ground.

"It – it was fine," Milly said a little breathlessly. She had feared that she might be air-sick, but the thrill of watching the tiny human figures in the sunlit fields, and town after town as they circled above them, with some new interest constantly arising out of the far horizon had made her completely forget her fear after the first few moments. Her cheeks were glowing now with a gentle flush from the swift wind of their flight, and her blue eyes were sparkling in her delicate little face with happy exhilaration.

The passage above well illustrates how Wheatley could build in his detailed knowledge of a locality, in this case gained both from his school days in Margate and subsequent return visits to the area throughout his life. Unfortunately, to the modern reader his narrative is very dated and his dialogue stilted to say the least, which is mostly why his books have all but disappeared in our day. In fact, he never completely got the hang of good dialogue, and in this example parts of Milly's speech sound almost like the transcription of a tourist pamphlet. Additionally, the burgeoning love interest here, which could have come straight out of a Mills & Boon romance, and which, as a general feature in all his novels, made his books so popular with women as well as with men, would no doubt be simply written off today derisively as 'cheesy'. However, in spite of there being many unappealing aspects for the modern reader in Wheatley's novels, their sense of place still very much endures and his depiction of the local area in *Contraband* remains as worth reading as ever.

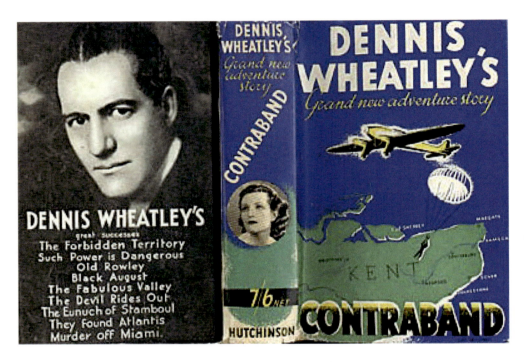

The cover of the First edition published 9 October 1936. It was originally serialised in an abridged form from 24 September to 3 November 1936 in the *Daily Mail*

CHAPTER TWELVE

BONDLAND

IAN FLEMING

Ian Fleming (1908 – 1964) had so many connections with Kent that the Isle of Thanet would inevitably flash through his highly-charged writing at some point. Fleming loved to drive down to Sandwich from London to play golf at the Royal St George's Golf Club, where he was a committee member, and in one of his best known stories, *Goldfinger*, this golfing interest translated itself into a classic match between James Bond and the villain Auric Goldfinger in Sandwich at the club Fleming renames as the Royal St Marks. In this novel Bond stays at a hotel in Ramsgate before heading on to Sandwich: clearly Fleming's knowledge of the south coast of Kent came in very handy for his storytelling.

Ian Fleming

Although Fleming never lived in Thanet, he knew it well enough and often passed by as he went, not only to to Sandwich, but also to St Margaret's Bay near Dover. He had a holiday home in St Margaret's Bay, a house called *White Cliffs*, which he bought from Noel Coward in 1952 and descended on for relaxation and entertaining over more than a decade. In later life he was a visitor to Higham Park at Bridge and between 1960 – 62 he owned the Old Palace at Bekesbourne, near Canterbury. In the area, the Duck Inn at Pett Bottom was one of Fleming's favourite locals. And we have the oft quoted fact that the London to Dover coach was the number 007. Like Dennis Wheatley (see Chapter Eleven), Fleming was no literary genius, but his storytelling, full of authentic details from the secret service, was compelling and, most of all, his creation of James Bond, at a time when the British Empire was breathing its last, was a brilliant piece of British wish fulfilment. In Bond he presented a British super hero who could defeat the foreign powers of evil (they are always foreign), a secret agent licensed to kill, allowed to act and behave above mundane morality and the petty social conventions of suburban man's everyday life. A huge excitement for twentieth century, post-war readers to enjoy in the safe comfort of their homes. Thanks to the films, which themselves have spawned ever more stories based on Fleming's ideas, this excitement has never waned.

In the *Goldfinger* story we now find Bond motoring down to Goldfinger's base at Reculver, on the Thanet border, then on to Ramsgate and finally Sandwich. En route, he indulges in an outrageous piece of driving by powering past a car that is holding him up on the inside. Another glorious, if totally reprehensible, piece of wish fulfilment.

From *Goldfinger* (1959):

Now Bond was running through the endless orchards of the Faversham growers. The sun had come out from behind the smog of London. There was the distant gleam of the Thames on his left. There was traffic on the river—long, glistening tankers, stubby merchantmen, antediluvian Dutch Schuyts. Bond left the Canterbury road and switched on to the incongruously rich highway that runs through the cheap bungaloid world of the holiday lands—Whitstable, Herne Bay, Birchington, Margate. He still idled along at fifty, holding the racing wheel on a light rein, listening to the relaxed purr of the exhausts, fitting the bits of his thoughts into the jigsaw as he had done two nights before with Goldfinger's face on the Identicast.

And, Bond reflected, while Goldfinger was pumping a million, two million pounds a year into the bloody maw of SMERSH, he was pyramiding his reserves, working on them, making them work for him whenever the odds were right, piling up the surplus for the day when the trumpets would sound in the Kremlin and every golden sinew would be mobilized. And no one outside Moscow had been watching the process, no one suspected that Goldfinger—the jeweller, the metallurgist, the resident of Reculver and Nassau, the respected member of Blades, of the Royal St Marks at Sandwich—was one of the greatest conspirators of all time, that he had financed the murder of hundreds, perhaps thousands of victims of SMERSH all over the world. SMERSH, 'Smiert Spionam', Death to Spies—the murder Apparat of the High Praesidium! And only M suspected it, only Bond knew it. And here was Bond, launched against this man by a series of flukes, a train of coincidence that had been started by a plane breaking down on the other side of the world. Bond smiled grimly to himself. How often in his profession had it been the same—the tiny acorn of coincidence that soared into the mighty oak whose branches darkened the sky. And now, once again, he was setting out to bring the dreadful growth down. With what? A bag of golf clubs?

A repainted sky-blue Ford Popular with large yellow ears was scurrying along the crown of the road ahead. Mechanically Bond gave the horn ring a couple of short, polite jabs. There was no reaction. The Ford Popular was doing its forty. Why should anyone want to go more than that respectable speed? The Ford obstinately hunched its shoulders and kept on its course. Bond gave it a sharp blast, expecting it to swerve. He had to touch his brakes when it didn't. Damn the man! Of course! The usual tense figure, hands held too high up on the wheel, and the inevitable hat, this time a particularly hideous black bowler, square on a large bullet head. Oh well, thought Bond, they weren't *his* stomach ulcers. He changed down and contemptuously slammed the D.B.III past on the inside. Silly bastard!

Another five miles and Bond was through the dainty teleworld of Herne Bay. The howl of Manston sounded away on his right. A flight of three Super Sabres came in to land. They skimmed below his right-hand horizon as if they were diving into the earth. With half his mind, Bond heard the roar of their jets catch up with them as they landed and taxied in to the hangars. He came up with a crossroads. To the left the signpost said RECULVER. Underneath was the ancient monument sign for Reculver church. Bond slowed, but didn't stop. No hanging about. He motored slowly on, keeping his eyes open. The shoreline was too exposed for a trawler to do anything but beach or anchor. Probably Goldfinger had used Ramsgate. Quiet little port. Customs and police who were probably only on the look-out for brandy coming over from France. There was a thick clump of trees between the road and the shore, a glimpse of roofs and of a medium-sized factory chimney with a thin plume of light smoke or steam. That would be it. Soon there was the gate of a long drive. A discreetly authoritative sign said THANET ALLOYS, and underneath: NO ADMITTANCE EXCEPT ON BUSINESS. All very respectable. Bond drove slowly on. There was nothing more to be seen. He took the next right-hand turn across the Manston plateau to Ramsgate. It was twelve o'clock. Bond inspected his room, a double with bathroom, on the top floor of the Channel Packet, unpacked his few belongings and went down to the snack bar where he had one vodka and tonic and two rounds of excellent ham sandwiches with plenty of mustard. Then he got back into his car and drove slowly over to the Royal St Marks at Sandwich.

The Royal St George's Golf Club, Sandwich, renamed as Royal St Marks

This passage shows how often Fleming had made the same journey described by Bond, a reflection of how every relevant detail from Fleming's real life experience was grist to his writing mill: Kent, including the Isle of Thanet, as seen here, as well as other obvious examples throughout the novels such as his wartime work in naval intelligence and his post as director of operations of the commando unit known as 30 Assault Unit, his membership of exclusive London clubs, and real people's names he came across, including, rather significantly, that of the American ornithologist James Bond, plus those of some boys he remembered from preparatory school days, allegedly bullies, with the surnames of Blofeld and Scaramanga. Fleming may have died prematurely in Canterbury in 1964 at the age of fifty-six, no doubt succumbing to the consequence of so many real-life vodka martinis and so much heavy smoking, but his alter ego, now almost elevated from fiction to reality, shows no sign of hanging up his Walther PPK and shuffling off his dangerous coil, even if his incursions into Thanet are now part of a distant past.

CHAPTER THIRTEEN

THIS ISLE, THIS ENGLAND

JOHN BETJEMAN

There is something so beautifully English about **Sir John Betjeman CBE** (1906 – 1984), a writer and poet who radiates an enthusiasm for English landscape, architecture and so many everyday details of the English way of life that perhaps only someone whose family came to England from another country could feel in such abundance. Could this champion of England really be descended from Dutch forbears, whose name, Betjemann, underwent a slight modification in England during the First World War to make it sound less Germanic? Born in London, he certainly lived the English dream, going on from Prep School to Marlborough College and thence to Magdalen College, Oxford (even though he left without a degree). And then in later life he looked so English, slightly old-fogeyish in his unobtrusive suit and trilby, an image which he, in fact, cultivated very carefully.

John Betjeman

During the Second World War, Betjeman worked for the films division of the Ministry of Information, also becoming British press attaché in neutral Dublin, Ireland, a post in which he is remembered as having acquitted himself well. And of course it was during the war years that he wrote his poem, *Margate 1940*, a poem that expressed through its evocation of the Isle's probably best-known seaside resort the very Englishness of England, and everything that was worth fighting for in those uncertain times. As well as capturing the flavour of a Margate seaside holiday, Betjeman shows how well he could observe his familiar surroundings and make them wonderfully meaningful. No metaphysical worries here, no foreign quotations, no precious flights of fancy, just simple but telling images of places and common objects with straightforward rhyme and metre. No wonder fellow poet Philip Larkin thought his poetry so much more worthwhile than the abstract, blank verse, angst of a great many modern poets of his time.

Margate 1940:

>From out The Queen's Highcliffe for weeks at a stretch
>I watched how the mower evaded the vetch,
>So that over the putting-course rashes were seen
>Of pink and of yellow among the burnt green.
>
>How restful to putt, when the strains of a band
>Announced a *thé dansant* was on at The Grand,
>While over the privet, commingalingly clear,
>I heard lesser Co-Optimists down by the pier.
>
>How lightly municipal, meltingly tarr'd,
>Were the walks through the lawns by the Queen's Promenade
>As soft over Cliftonville languished the light
>Down Harold Road, Norfolk Road, into the night.
>
>Oh! then what a pleasure to see the ground floor
>With tables for two laid as tables for four,
>And bottles of sauce and *Kia-Ora* and squash
>Awaiting their owners who'd gone up to wash -

Who had gone up to wash the ozone from their skins
The sand from their legs and the rock from their chins,
To prepare for an evening of dancing and cards
And forget the sea-breeze on the dry promenades.

From third floor and fourth floor the children looked down
Upon ribbons of light in the salt-scented town;
And drowning the trams roared the sound of the sea
As it washed in the shingle the scraps of their tea.

Beside The Queen's Highcliffe now rank grows the vetch,
Now dark is the terrace, a storm-battered stretch;
And I think, as the fairy-lit sights I recall,
It is those we are fighting for, foremost of all.

Betjeman was a man steeped in the past, albeit a recent past, with a distinct dislike of modernity. This dislike shines out in so much of his writing, perhaps most famously in his poem *Slough*, a town that had recently undergone modernization and become overridden with hundreds of new factories ('Come, friendly bombs, and fall on Slough!'). But perhaps nowhere is this feel for the recent past, with its small, modest and very English pleasures, as warmly felt as in his poem about Margate, written when the resort of old had fallen quiet and the darkness of war had descended on the fondly remembered but now empty holiday town. It is only when we are in danger of losing the familiar enjoyments of our country, Betjeman tells us, that we realize how much they form part of our national heritage and are worth fighting for 'foremost of all'.

The two hotels in Cliftonville, Margate that later merged into The Queen's Highcliffe

PAUL THEROUX

It would take another person from abroad, but newly arrived this time, to create an updated feel for the Isle of Thanet in the twentieth century. **Paul Theroux** (1941 -), an American writer of huge wit and perspicuity, and the author of many acclaimed novels such as *The Mosquito Coast*, decided one fine day, while resident in London in the 1980s, to walk around the British Isles and write up his impressions of Britain's coastal life. He began in Margate. His resulting book, *The Kingdom by the Sea*, combined an interest in all things British with a fine, sometimes very incisive, style of humour. The book is neither a novel nor a poetic evocation, and so the following extract departs somewhat from the writings included

Paul Theroux

hitherto, except perhaps those of Daniel Defoe, but neither is it just a travelogue. It is a journey, a compelling narrative and piece of literary humour all combined and its sharpness of observation surely warrants its inclusion as a still fresh and relatively modern view of the Isle.

Here we join Theroux as he leaves Cliftonville, Margate, and makes his way to Broadstairs.

From *The Kingdom By The Sea* (1983):

I climbed some stairs that passed through a 'gate' – a cut – in the chalk cliffs and then walked along the path at the top to Cliftonville. This was a sedate suburb of Margate, full of small damp bungalows and ragged sparrows. A hawk flew slowly near the edge of the cliff, and the gulls nagged nearer the sea. It was not quiet, what with the gulls and the surf sighing, and the wind scraping the hedges, but it was noisy in a peaceful way.

Many signs said DANGEROUS CLIFFS and warned walkers not to go too close to the edge. The chalk was collapsing, and I could see that large bluffs had toppled to the shore. It reminded me that in the few coastal parts of Britain where I had hiked there had been signs warning of breaking cliffs and unsafe paths. What I had seen of the Dorset coast was slipping into the Channel:

portions of pasture-land and meadows had fallen, and the fences had gone with them in a tangle of posts and wire. These chalk cliffs of Kent – so white and sturdy when seen from a distance – were frail and friable, and this coast made Britain seem like a country consisting of stale cake that softened and broke in the rain.

The rain was patchy. I saw through its drapes two blind men – one black, one white – being led along the path by two sighted ladies. The black man said, 'Just how wide is it?' The white one said, 'The dogs need a little space to play.' A pair of dogs trotted behind this party, and the men tapped their canes as they went past me. Farther on, I heard music. It was 'We'll Gather Lilacs in the Spring Again', being played by a man seated at an organ in an open-air amphitheatre. The wind shipped at the folding chairs around him and made their canvas flutter and flap. There were more than five hundred chairs, and all of them were empty. The man went on playing and pulling out stops while the chairs flapped under the grey sky. I continued down the path, along the cloud-mottled water of the sea, and on this drab afternoon I heard a nightingale singing in a hedge. 'The nightingale sings of adulterous wrong.' T. S. Eliot was here having a mild nervous breakdown in 1921, staying at the Albemarle Hotel right over there in Cliftonville.

The sun came out as I walked along the North Foreland, past Kingsgate with its small pretty cove and its modern castle on one bluff, and a handsome lighthouse like a white pepper-mill just behind it on a higher point of land. There were cooing doves in the trees and the high box hedges of the big houses were like fortifications.

Only four miles from Margate and it was the England of fresh paint and flower gardens and tall chimneys. And there was a clearer intimation of this area's respectability: this road smelled of private schools – it was a certain kind of soap and a certain kind of cooking, and the sound of young voices and laughter coming from the open windows of large rooms. An hour ago it had been Skinheads and chip-shops and rain on Margate Sands, and now this breezy bourgeois headland in bright sunshine, as I approached Broadstairs. I thought: Mexico is one landscape – one visible thing – and all of Arabia is one thing; but I began to suspect that every mile of England was different.

Broadstairs was full of flesh-coloured flowers. There were no Skinheads here, no Nazi slogans, no signs saying *Anarchy!* - that was always a popular one in public toilets in England. There were about thirty Mods drinking cider on the front, passing half-gallon bottles back and forth. These boys had removed their jackets and crash helmets and shirts, and they sat in the sun on the green park benches. There was no loud music, no honky-tonk, at Broadstairs; the front was genteel – the iron ornateness of Victorian porches.

'Charles Dickens lived in this house', the sign said on a brick house, with a brick turret, that was smack on the coastal path at the edge of Broadstairs. Dickens had said that Broadstairs beat 'all watering-places into what the Americans call "sky-blue fits"'. This residence had been given the name 'Bleak House' and in its gift shop it was possible to buy pot-holders and tea towels and key chains stamped *Bleak House – Broadstairs*. Upstairs, the novelist's desk and wash basin were on view and could be seen for a small charge. It was of particular interest to me that Dickens had written most of *American Notes* in this house. He sat at this desk and looked out of that window and dipped this pen in that ink-pot and wrote, 'To represent me as viewing America with ill-nature, coldness or animosity, is merely to do a very foolish thing, which is always a very easy one.'

There was a fortune-teller's shop on the front at Broadstairs, with a sign saying *Olandah Clairvoyante*. She was said to be the wisest woman in Europe. A testimonial letter taped on to her window said, 'Dear Olandah, Whenever I feel depressed, which is every day, I take your letter out and read it and feel so much better - .'

Which is every day? I went into the shop. Olandah was seated behind a curtain. She wore a scarf on her head and what looked like stage make-up and beads. Her expression was full of weary suspicion and she stared with such seriousness I thought she had terrible news for me.

'She said, 'Do you want a reading?'

I said yes. She took my hand loosely, as if weighing it to bite. She said I was far from home – had my knapsack and muddy shoes given her a clue? She said I was doing a very difficult thing, but if she was referring to travelling around Britain perhaps she knew something I didn't, because I had not foreseen any difficulties. She said I was sensitive and artistic: perhaps a painter? 'Couldn't draw a rabbit,' I said. She said I was successful but that I tried to hide it. I was often in the company of strangers. Some of them would try to take advantage of me, but my character would overcome them.

All this she gathered by prodding the palm of my right hand and tracing her crimson fingernails on the lines I got from rowing a skiff in Cape Cod Bay.

'Do you see anything there about Northern Ireland?'

'Distant lands certainly. One of them might be Ulster.'

'Do I survive in the end?'

'Oh, yes. You lead a healthy life. You are not a smoker, for example.'

'Gave up a year ago. Pipe. I used to inhale it. I miss it sometimes like a dead friend.'

'You have many friends,' Olandah said, perhaps mishearing me. 'But you tend to keep away from them. You keep yourself to yourself. You are very independent.'

'Self-employed,' I said. 'One last query. Where am I going to sleep tonight?'

She stopped looking at my hand. She looked at my nose and said, 'Not at home.'

'What town – can you give me a hint?'

'I give character readings, ' Olandah said. 'I don't give tourist information.'

This cost me seven pounds, which was about a pound more than it would have cost me to stay at a guest house, with bed and breakfast. Still, I was grateful for her encouragement and glad to have been reassured that I was going to survive.

Another sign in Broadstairs said, 'Seven miles out to sea from this point lie the dreaded Goodwin Sands – the great ship swallower – considered by a great many seafarers to be the most dangerous stretch of water in the world.' There were countless stories about the disasters and wrecks on the Goodwins. 'Their ingurgitating property is such, that a vessel of the largest size, driven upon them, would in a few days be swallowed up and seen no more.' What was not so well known was that at the turn of the century, at low water, the sands became very firm and cricket matches were played on them.

The site of Olandah's former kiosk on Broadstairs seafront

As Theroux's observations show, it is impossible to avoid depicting the decline that Margate had entered into in the 1980s and the contrast with leafier Broadstairs. Of course, Theroux's writing itself betrays the very irony and impish humour that is so characteristic of

English writing of this period and which continues with us to this day. Nonetheless, all those familiar with the Isle, and especially those whose memories go back to the 1980s, will appreciate the aptness of his remarks and description, even if sometimes, like Defoe's at the very beginning of this literary odyssey, they are hardly the comments that might be made in a tourist leaflet. But at least his focus on the Goodwin Sands at the end links us back to our earlier literary friends, Wilkie Collins and R M Ballantyne. Some aspects of the Isle never change and remain a constant in every kind of writer.

AFTERWORD

T S Eliot, while recuperating in Cliftonville in 1921, as noted by Paul Theroux above, brought Margate incidentally into his great culturally meditative poem *The Wasteland* with the words:

> On Margate sands.
> I can connect
> Nothing with nothing.

This walk-on part for Margate in the long sweep of the poem mirrored his earlier minor character creation J Alfred Prufrock, an unobtrusive man who was no Prince Hamlet but one that would do to 'swell a progress, start a scene or two'. In the same way as Margate in Eliot's poem, and Prufrock before, the Isle of Thanet as a whole has until recently largely played an incidental role, starting a scene or two, in the grand scheme of the literary works in which it figured.

But things have changed. Now, in the twenty-first century, it might be truer to say that the isle has risen from supporting role to fully-fledged star, becoming not only the entire setting for an array of modern novels but an integral part of their composition. Transformed from Prufrock into Citizen Kane.

Perhaps the first pointer to this change came at the end of the twentieth century with Bruce Robinson's 1997 semi-autobiographical novel *The Peculiar Memories of Thomas Penman*. Robinson, script-writer of the award-winning film *The Killing Fields* and both writer and director of the widely lauded black comedy film *Withnail and I*, created in his novel a fictionalized memoir which evokes the very flavour, taste and feel of Broadstairs, the Thanet town he grew up in during the 1950s. Those who know the town instantly recognize the names of streets, the houses, the beaches, even the vicarage in St Peters, and anyone whose early years were in Thanet will identify with at least some of the experiences and memories of seaside life of the young protagonist of the book.

The growing trend to make the Isle of Thanet the whole setting and central feature of recent literary endeavours is due in good part to a number of significant contemporary writers either being from Thanet, like Robinson, or coming to take up permanent residence on the isle rather than just paying temporary visits. There were already glimpses of things to come in the shape of Orczy's novel *The Nest of the Sparrowhawk* set in Acol, thanks to the author's three-year stay in Thanet (see Chapter Eight), and, of course, Frank Richards, creator of Billy Bunter, incorporated many features of Thanet into his Greyfriars stories once he had moved permanently to Kingsgate (see Chapter Ten).

One contemporary author who in fact matched both criteria of being from Thanet and also living permanently on the isle was the brilliantly witty Jane Wenham-Jones, now sadly, and prematurely, deceased. The first of her wonderfully humorous books, *Raising The Roof,* was published at the very beginning of this century, in 2001. Wenham-Jones sets this story about money-making schemes entirely in Ramsgate, based on her own buy-to-let experience. Later books were set in her home town of Broadstairs. In *One Glass Is Never Enough* (2005), she clearly uses for material her own co-ownership of a wine bar in Broadstairs, and again *The Big Five-O* (2019), a very feminine take on hitting the age of fifty, is explicitly located and narrated in her home town.

Like many on the Isle of Thanet, Wenham-Jones began life by teaching English to the legions of foreign students who, pre-pandemic, came to the many language schools on the isle. For several decades foreign students were a distinct feature of life in modern Thanet and it is rare to find any local person who has not in some way been involved with this enterprise, either at an educational or accommodation level. It is hopefully permissible therefore for the author of this current book, who has lived on the isle since the early 1980s, to make reference to his own semi-autobiographical novel centred on running a language school in the seaside town of Bradgate (a Buchanesque reference to *The Thirty-Nine Steps* here, see Chapter Nine), entitled *The English Chronicles* (2018).

Another author to set their work entirely in Thanet is the widely-known London-based novelist, Sophia Tobin, who, like Bruce Robinson, grew up on the Isle of Thanet. She is the author of several acclaimed novels and in her 2015 novel, *The Widow's Confession*, she has set the narrative entirely in Broadstairs. Or at least, the Broadstairs of 1851. It is a mystery story with both historical and thriller elements, leading one critic to link it with that other Thanet-associated author, Wilkie Collins (see Chapter Six).

The Thanet of today takes centre stage again for Maggie Gee's 2019 novel, *Blood*. This novel filled with black humour and *de rigueur* expletives is an up-to-the-minute, larger-than-life whodunnit framed by vivid descriptions of the locations, characters, streets, events and even shops that make up the isle, with a bit of extra depth lent by reference to writers like Coleridge who are associated with the area. The book is in some ways a homage to Thanet by a well-known modern novelist, the author of fifteen widely lauded books, who has left London in recent years to make her permanent home in Ramsgate.

There continue to be Thanet episodes of varying degree in contemporary novels, such as Clare Chambers' beautifully evoked story of ordinary life in the 1950s, *Small Pleasures* (2020), where the nursing home for youngsters is located in Broadstairs, and Lynne Francis' historical novel *A Maid's Ruin* (2020), which starts off in Margate (and has the alternative title *The Margate Maid*). But these episodes are now eclipsed by the full frontal use of

Thanet in so many new novels, and the newest, perhaps the most notable of these to illuminate the trend, is *Dreamland* by Rosa Rankin-Gee, which appeared in 2021.

Rankin-Gee has followed her novelist mother Maggie Gee, and historian father Nicholas Rankin, from London to Thanet and is able to give a very young, streetwise view of Thanet in this acclaimed book, her second novel. In fact, the story is set in the near future, where climate change has caused a breakdown in government and law and order, and the rising sea levels have given rise to a chilling policy of creating a Trump-like wall around the isle and imprisoning the unproductive inhabitants on the island, which really is becoming an island again, and leaving them to their fate. The protagonist lives in Margate with her dysfunctional mother and we are given a no-holds-barred description, with matching dialogue, of a Margate enmeshed in alcohol, drugs and crime. It is a startling evocation, with page-turning suspense, in full dystopian mode, where the only way forward finally is escape from Thanet over the wall.

But the past tells us that this is not the last word on Thanet, and that soon there will be more words to continue writing the isle into literary history.